R3 Corda for Architects and Developers

With Case Studies in Finance, Insurance, Healthcare, Travel, Telecom, and Agriculture

Debajani Mohanty

Apress®

R3 Corda for Architects and Developers

Debajani Mohanty
Noida, Uttar Pradesh, India

ISBN-13 (pbk): 978-1-4842-4531-6   ISBN-13 (electronic): 978-1-4842-4529-3
https://doi.org/10.1007/978-1-4842-4529-3

Managing Director, Apress Media LLC: Welmoed Spahr
Acquisitions Editor: Celestin Suresh John
Development Editor: Siddhi Chavan
Coordinating Editor: Aditee Mirashi

Cover designed by eStudioCalamar

Cover image designed by Freepik (www.freepik.com)

Distributed to the book trade worldwide by Springer Science+Business Media New York, 233 Spring Street, 6th Floor, New York, NY 10013. Phone 1-800-SPRINGER, fax (201) 348-4505, e-mail orders-ny@springer-sbm.com, or visit www.springeronline.com. Apress Media, LLC is a California LLC and the sole member (owner) is Springer Science + Business Media Finance Inc (SSBM Finance Inc). SSBM Finance Inc is a **Delaware** corporation.

For information on translations, please e-mail rights@apress.com, or visit http://www.apress.com/rights-permissions.

Apress titles may be purchased in bulk for academic, corporate, or promotional use. eBook versions and licenses are also available for most titles. For more information, reference our Print and eBook Bulk Sales web page at http://www.apress.com/bulk-sales.

Any source code or other supplementary material referenced by the author in this book is available to readers on GitHub via the book's product page, located at www.apress.com/978-1-4842-4531-6. For more detailed information, please visit http://www.apress.com/source-code.

Printed on acid-free paper

Table of Contents

TABLE OF CONTENTS

v

About the Author

Debajani Mohanty, author of the Amazon bestsellers *BlockChain: From Concept to Execution* (BPB Publications, 2018), *Ethereum for Architects and Developers* (Apress, 2019), and now *R3 Corda for Architects and Developers*, is a Solution Architect with close to 18 years of experience in the industry. Her books have been translated into German and Chinese. Debajani is a keynote speaker at Philadelphia PACT, NASSCOM, IIM, WomenWhoCode, Unicom, Amity, India International Centre, and many similar national and international tech events. She is Honorary Faculty with Amity University, consultant, and an advisor and mentor to numerous reputed organizations in India and abroad. Debajani is also a woman activist and writer felicitated by Nobel laureate Kailash Satyarthi for her outstanding contributions to woman empowerment in India.

Follow her on Twitter: `https://twitter.com/debimr75`

Follow her on LinkedIn: `https://www.linkedin.com/in/debajanimohantypmp/`

About the Technical Reviewer

 **Prem Naraindas** is a hands-on and highly experienced technology executive with over 17 years of successful, enterprise-level accomplishments with a passion to drive customer engagements to successful outcomes from start to finish. Through the course of his career, Prem has led transformational initiatives for clients in areas such as application development and maintenance, business process outsourcing, engineering services, R&D, innovation, and infrastructure. Prem has over three years of experience with Enterprise Blockchain, has been responsible for delivering over 20 Proofs of Concept, and has successfully envisaged and led production implementation of one of the world's first Enterprise Blockchain applications. In his current role, Prem is Global Blockchain Offering Director at DXC technology. This role is part of the DXC Global Blockchain Practice, in which Prem is responsible for understanding the Enterprise Blockchain market demands and trends and for working with clients, sales teams, delivery, and consultants to make the strategy relevant to DXC's client base and to create Blockchain offerings and solutions with value superior to that offered by the competition. He is also responsible for understating the market dynamics to drive DXC's Blockchain product, platform development, and go-to-market strategies.

Acknowledgments

This book is possible because of the combined effort of many; my work is so small it causes only ripples in a massive ocean. I take this opportunity to offer my gratitude to the following people for always being there with me when I was in need: my grandmother Mrs. Renuka Das, mother Mrs. Nirupama Mohanty, father Dr. N. K. Mohanty, husband Dr. Rajul Rastogi, and uncle Dr. N. R. Das. I am also grateful to Prem Naraindas, DXC Technology for taking his valuable time to review this book on time.

Last but not least, thanks to Coordinating Editor Aditee Mirashi, Acquisitions Editor Celestin Suresh John at Apress; for all the help while working on the book.

Introduction

R3 Corda for Architects and Developers is intended to be the standard book on R3 Corda, the industry-leading distributed ledger technology (DLT). The book explores the entire Corda ecosystem step by step with adequate theory, labs, and live use cases.

Today, R3 Corda has emerged as the DLT platform of choice for the insurance domain as well as many banks and regtech organizations. The main issue learning R3 Corda is the lack of trainers and the scarcity of sample codes in a well-accepted language such as Java, since most of its existing examples are written in Kotlin. *R3 Corda for Architects and Developers* will fill that vacuum by providing contents suitable to all stakeholders consolidated in one place. In this reading journey, the reader will be introduced chapter by chapter to Blockchain concepts, DLT, R3 Corda architecture, and smart contract programming in Java with ample examples, guiding the reader through testing and deployment of the entire ecosystem. In later chapters, readers will be introduced to various business problems in healthcare, agriculture, and a few other domains and how Corda can solve these issues through its unique and efficient DLT offering. The book also provides sample codes of some useful Proof of Concepts (PoCs) that will be most benefical to business leaders and architects in their Corda journey from concept to execution. The business scenarios and solutions are provided with flowcharts, diagrams, and sample codes that stakeholders can refer to, further enhance as per their respective business needs, and deploy in live projects.

The book will be very useful for readers of every background, whether they are eager to develop decentralized applications in R3 Corda, or wish to learn its architecture, or even are interested in exploring different use cases that can be implemented using this technology across business verticals. By the end of the book, readers will have enough information about how the correct usage of R3 Corda can create value for their business processes by eliminating middleman costs and bringing in transparency for creation of deduplicated, fraud-proof data storage for smoother execution of business. The best and most unique part of the book is that all the examples are written in Java.

Readership (who's the target audience?):

The book will appeal to the novice who wishes to learn R3 Corda from scratch and continue the journey until he or she knows the whole ecosystem and is able to deploy code in production. At the same time, it will be of interest to an existing Blockchain developer or architect, to know the R3 Corda best practices and live use cases where R3 Corda can do its wonders by bringing transparency to processes, cutting middleman costs, reducing time of operation, and finally eliminating fraud and duplication of data.

CHAPTER 1

Barter to Blockchain

In childhood, I heard many stories from my legendary grandfather about how certain people created immense amount of wealth in a short time, of course in an honest way, and then more importantly how they kept it all safe. While most little girls of my age were fascinated by fairytale stories, I found wealth creation ideas much more alluring and a means to be a powerful someone someday later in life. With time I came to know I was not the only one in this game. People in all ages and all times have ceaselessly thought over this puzzle of "creating wealth," "securing it," and "trading or investing for larger returns." Be it gold, spices, cattle, slaves, land, or oil, wealth has many different forms and there are inherent flaws when it comes to trading in wealth. In this chapter, let's discuss some of the different forms of money and figure out how this journey finally culminated in Bitcoin and Blockchain, one of the biggest technical inventions of the 21st century.

History of Money

Have you ever wondered why we need to secure our valuables, and if so was there always a need to do so? Well, perhaps not. More than ten thousand years back, human beings lived in caves. They were hunters who lived on their daily earnings, whether animal or fruit or equivalent, and there was no need to store or keep such perishable items safe for a long time. That was the time when they started living in groups in caves to

© Debajani Mohanty 2019
D. Mohanty, *R3 Corda for Architects and Developers*,
https://doi.org/10.1007/978-1-4842-4529-3_1

stay protected from animal attacks and other natural calamities. Slowly, they gained different skills such as cooking, making weapons, and sewing clothes. Gradually they learned cultivation and domestication of certain animals. Soon people started a classification and division of labor on the basis of specialization of skills, so that a particular group of people good at a certain skill would work in that particular skill area only. However, that led to a problem: for example let's say a farmer who cultivated rice produced more rice than his family could consume and at the same time needed milk for his family. Where would this farmer be able to get it? So the need to trade took a concrete shape. Some 9,000 to 10,000 years back, people started trading, and the mechanism is called "the barter system." This is a very popular mechanism to exchange products and services and people even today do it in every country in the world.

Barter System

The barter system, the most primeval form of trading, was easy and simple. People used to gather in groups on a particular day and exchange items for something else that would be useful for them. Mostly it was an exchange of products and services, which happens even today in many communities and countries across the world. The barter system gained wide popularity because of its simple way of exchanging products and services. However, the double coincidence of wants was always a problem. For example, there might not be an exact requirement match of commodities between parties. Divisibility too was another concern. Let's consider an example; one cow is selling for ten chickens. However, what if someone wants to purchase only one chicken. Also commodities were mostly perishable items and could not be stored as permanent wealth. So there was a need for a universally approved token that could be used as an exchange item for payment and would address the original issues inherent in the "barter system" of that time: divisibility, perishability, exchangeability, storage, and so on.

Metal Currency

So some people who had understood the limitations of the barter system started thinking of an alternate payment medium and that is the time when metal currency was introduced. At different time periods, different types of currencies were in execution: for example, grains, seashells, leather money, and so on. Finally metal currencies were introduced between 700 BC and 600 BC. In order to make the currency universal, these metal currencies needed approval or stamp by kings and rulers. Initially, only those metals that were durable, divisible, portable, limited in supply, and nonperishable were selected. Also, it's very important that in terms of weight and value, the price of metal was the price of money so that even if someone used regular silver or gold to create fake currencies it would not affect the monetary valuation system. The issue with metal currencies was that they were heavy and difficult to transport in larger quantities. Also, the utility of metals was wasted by converting them to currency.

Paper Money

Time and need again prompted certain smart people to craft another currency which would be lighter and easier for storage and would have no intrinsic value so that metals and usable items can be saved for utility. Hence paper money was introduced somewhere around 800–900 AD. However, the issue with paper money was that it could be quickly reproduced in an illegal way, and also that it could be misused by black-marketers and money-hoarders. The most dangerous part, however, was that it carried no inherent value.

Banks

Over the last few thousand years, banks have evolved to a great extent; however modern banks mostly have the same operations as centuries back: credit and debit. Banks will take the money that users deposit, invest it elsewhere, get some profits, and return back the principal with interest to the users. Also, after paper money was introduced, banks played a central role in guaranteeing the value of money. The emblem that kings and rulers once enforced to convert a metal to a currency nowadays is done by the banks.

With time, banks mushroomed everywhere, and gradually every country appointed a central bank to regulate functions of banks and act as the centralized authority to carry out monetary policy, taxation, and economic development of the country. The following are some examples of central banks:

- Reserve Bank of India, India

- Federal Reserve System, USA

- Bank of England, UK

Issue with Centralized Authority in Banking

Since our school days, our textbooks have taught us about monetary policies and claimed that banks are the safest place to save our hard-earned money. Let's find out the extent to which that's true. If you peruse the history of banking, you can find a plethora of financial crises: credit crisis in 1772, the Great Depression beginning in 1929, and the banking crisis in 2008, among others. During such a crisis, there is a sudden panic in the market followed by a long list of investors who wish to withdraw their investments from banks almost immediately. But banks might not always have a reserve of cash as they have invested it elsewhere; hence they are not in a position to handle paying back all deposits quickly if there is a sudden hike in demand. Under such instances, they declare bankruptcy.

It is interesting to note that such financial crises are mostly human created and might not have much to do with the inherent price of commodities. For example, if a seller wishes to sell a property in the market, then the cash amount that they would get would be different at different points of time depending upon the market conditions. However, if they want to exchange it with any commodity, for example a property owner in San Francisco wishes to exchange their house with another one in New York, the exchange rate might not vary unless there is again a mismatch between demand and supply. Hence, during many financial crises in history, it's observed that the age-old barter system has come back into the mainstream.

2008 Financial Crisis: A Pathbreaker

Among all these historical financial crises, the most recent one, which most of us have observed in our lifetimes, was in the year 2008. Who can forget its impact: so much unemployment, property meltdown and ill health? If one traces down what went wrong, it's pretty simple and it could have been completely avoided.

In the 2007–2008 time period, banks had started to give out risky loans to people even with bad credit history to attract new customers mostly out of greed for a possible higher interest rate. Ultimately, that money could not be paid back for obvious reasons. Many banks collapsed and filed for bankruptcy. The American government tried to save some financial institutions from crisis by bailing them out. However, money offered by the government to the banks was also the people's money, which had been paid in taxes. The actions of the American government led to customer dissatisfaction across the entire country. Since the global economy is interconnected and most banks work in brotherhood, the events that took place in the United States also affected the world, bringing the world's economy to a standstill.

Bitcoin Was Born

As in earlier phases in the evolution of money, after the 2008 financial crisis some intellectuals started doubting centralized systems as banks and financial organizations. Why?

- Banks might not be actually a trusted third party for securing all the money.

- Banks charge a huge fee for their services, especially for international remittances.

- They take considerable time for clearing transactions in interbank and intercountry transactions.

It's quite amusing that while in most countries in the world, democracy is prevalent in terms of choosing leadership, when it comes to money we still live in autocracy as the money is handled by banks, a centralized third party, rather than lying in the hands of the people.

In documented human history over the past thousand years, we have witnessed many demonetizations, where an existing currency is invalidated, followed by remonetization, in which a form of payment is restored as legal tender. Currencies were a mere representation of exchange media and yet carried no value without the backing of kings, emperors, or ruling governments.

Cryptocurrency is one such currency: its distribution and exchange though is entirely confined to the digital world. Contrary to the belief of many, Bitcoin is not the first cryptocurrency. DigiCash in 1992, CyberCash in 1994, E-Gold in 1996, WebMoney in 1998, Liberty Reserve in 2006, and Perfect Money in 2007 were all crypto or digital currencies, some of which are still in use by communities. However Bitcoin was revolutionary as it came up with a new, previously unseen concept: decentralization.

Note   While all these currencies are referred to as cryptocurrency, the regular currencies such as USD, GBP, INR, and so on are still known as fiat currencies or fiat cash.

Bitcoin White Paper

It's hard to believe the legendary cryptocurrency Bitcoin is only a decade old and only a baby in the world of money and yet could bring in such high value to the monetary system. In October 2008, Satoshi Nakamoto's nine-page Bitcoin white paper appeared on the market, and not too many paid attention. However, in just under a decade's time, this technology proved to be the most disruptive since the invention of the Internet itself. This white paper specified

- Instructions on how to run the Bitcoin network.

- Why and how transactions are hashed and saved to Merkle root (should be explained later in this Chapter).

- How network handles anticipatory attacks.

- How to establish a Proof-of-Work (PoW) system to deter hackers (should be explained later in this Chapter).

- How it is practically impossible for hackers to change transactions.

- How to prohibit double spending in a decentralized way not involving a centralized third party such as banks (should be explained later in this Chapter).

Why Bitcoin Took the Market by Storm

As discussed, over the last three or four decades, many people have tried their hands at digital or electronic currencies but failed due to technical or regulatory issues. So what value did Bitcoin bring that made the world go crazy over it?

The following are a few of its benefits:

- Immunity to fraud

- Low transaction fees

- Settlement in minutes

- Universally acceptable, well mostly

Over the years, the price of Bitcoin has gone on a roller coaster ride. While many countries such as the United States, Canada, and Australia, as well as the European Union and so on, have gladly and openly embraced Bitcoin, there are few who still have their inhibitions. I am hopeful that in our lifetimes a day will arrive when fiat currencies will be entirely replaced by their digital and crypto counterparts.

The most beautiful part of Bitcoin, however, is its underlying mechanism to store data that is immutable and immune to fraud, and to use cryptology in a secure way for sharing data across parties. This revolutionary new technology is called *Blockchain*. In other words, Bitcoin is peer-to-peer electronic cash that is more valuable than legacy systems due to the autonomous monetary benefits that it brings in a decentralized manner. Blockchain is the technology of storing records or data as blocks similar to linked lists that use cryptographic hashing algorithms and Merkle trees. We will cover more on this Chapter.

In the last decade, investment in Blockchain has increased exponentially. According to a new research report, "Blockchain-as-a-Service Market by Component (Tools and Services), Business Application (Supply Chain Management, Smart Contracts, Identity Management, Payments, and GRC Management), Organization Size, Industry, and

Region - Global Forecast to 2023," published by MarketsandMarkets, the market is expected to grow from USD 623.0 million in 2018 to USD 15,455 million by 2023, at a compound annual growth rate (CAGR) of 90.1% during the forecast period.

Introduction to Blockchain

Before we go any further, here are a few features to broadly define Blockchain:

- It's a distributed ledger or register over a public or private network.

- Every node in the network carries an exact replica of the ledger.

- Data on this ledger is secure because it's encrypted using private-key cryptography, which can be decrypted only with its matching public key.

- There is no single point of failure and no downtime.

- Data can be added with everyone's or a group's consensus rather than a centralized authority. Hence, it's called decentralized in terms of consensus.

- Data in Blockchain is immutable (i.e., once stored can't be altered).

- Each record in the database is known as a block; each block points to a previous block in the chain.

- Each new block consists of a group of transactions that is added to the end of a Blockchain.

- Smart contracts can run on this ledger, triggering programs to run automatically when a specific condition is met.

Blockchain is a distributed decentralized ledger (or database) where data can be added in append-only mode in a secure way. This ledger can be used by parties and organizations that do not trust each other for complex business transactions and can be treated as a single source of truth for all participating parties, as each will share a replica of the global data, just like others.

Just like artificial intelligence, IoT, virtual reality, and so on, Blockchain is an emerging technology, and being only a decade old, it's almost the youngest of all the other similar technologies. Please note that research in artificial intelligence got initiated back in 1950s–1960s, and now we are seeing its usage in the real world. However, in the case of Blockchain, adoption is happening with manifold speed.

In order to know Blockchain, we have to know how Bitcoin or Ethereum or any other similar public Blockchain network works. But first, let's find out the business problem that Blockchain can address.

Business Problem

Before learning Blockchain or distributed ledger technology (DLT) in detail, one may wonder why the market is so fascinated regarding Blockchain. If Blockchain is a storing mechanism, many such mechanisms have existed in industry for decades.

The answer is that Blockchain is not useful to store data for an individual, but is useful for multiple parties, especially those who do not trust each other and yet wish to share data for some business transaction.

So, let's find out about the different mechanisms used in the current market to allow enterprises as banks, financial organizations, and global distributed systems (GDS) in travel or supply chain systems to communicate with each other. Consider three independent organizations trying to do some business together for any vertical. Before their collaboration, they had their individual data in their respective silos. Now that they have come together, what are the possible ways to share data? Most organizations share data in two different ways: fully distributed model or fully centralized model. However, now we have a third model to explore: DLT, the decentralized peer-to-peer model, or Blockchain. Let's discuss them in detail.

Fully Distributed Model

Most of our current projects must be aligned with this model as specified in Figure 1-1, where each of the three organizations maintain their own data and communicate through some web service or messaging protocol. There could be many problems in such a process, and so let's look at a few of them:

- Most of the data would be redundant, with each organization carrying its own version.

- Data across organizations might not be in sync due to latency issues.

- Processes would be wasteful; reconciliations would be complex and expensive.

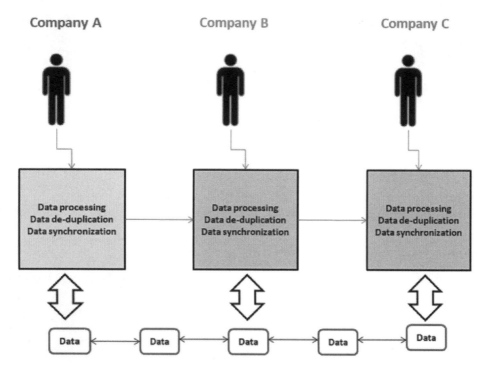

Figure 1-1. *Three organizations working in distributed mode of sharing data*

Fully Centralized Model

We have already found issues with a distributed system, so now how can we move to a completely shared model that would be secure and neutral for all these organizations? As shown in Figure 1-2, organizations achieve this mostly by delegating this responsibility to a third party that would work as a common platform for all parties to store and share data.

Let's explore issues here.

- This is an expensive way, as third parties will charge for such a service.

- They may have a conflict of interest with the individual organization. One or more of the parties may not agree on the data for some reason.

- There could be legal issues leading to data regulation.

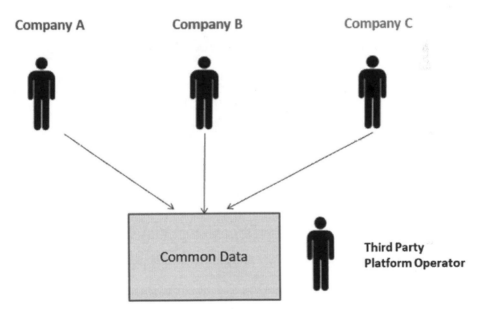

Figure 1-2. *Three organizations working in centralized mode of sharing data*

So what could be a model where parties can share data in the most efficient way so that the following conditions are met?

- Data at sync across all the network

- No or minimal redundancy

- Fewer expenses due to reconciliations and the like

- Easy auditing

The new mechanism that comes to mind is a DLT.

DLT, the Decentralized Peer-to-Peer Model

As shown in Figure 1-3, DLT is a mechanism that works in a peer-to-peer fashion that is different from the two previous models. Using DLT, we can develop applications and platforms where ownership is shared across the network of collaborating companies, completely eliminating the need for a third parties to operate the applications on your behalf.

- Mutual processes and data are shared as tamperproof single sources of truth that entirely remove the need for traditional integration, data translation, duplication, and redundancy.

- Data synchronization and consensus are provided by the DLT platform. Applications are built once in collaboration and used by many parties.

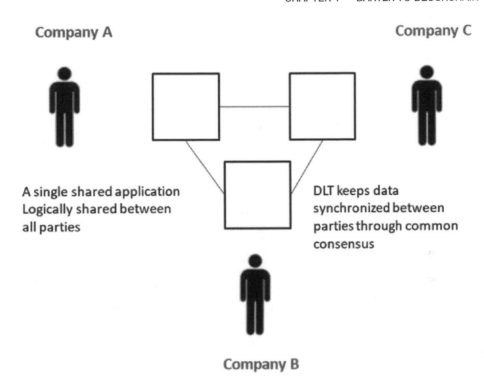

Figure 1-3. *Three organizations working in peer-to-peer mode of sharing data*

Now that you broadly know the three models, just see how nodes representing parties can be pictorially represented. Figure 1-4 is a pictorial comparison between centralized client/server and peer-to-peer models.

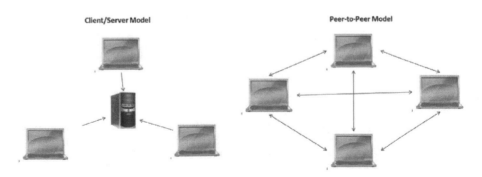

Figure 1-4. *Client/server vs. peer-to-peer model*

Now let's see how these two patterns can be further modified by bringing a higher intensity of decentralization to the overall network in Figure 1-5.

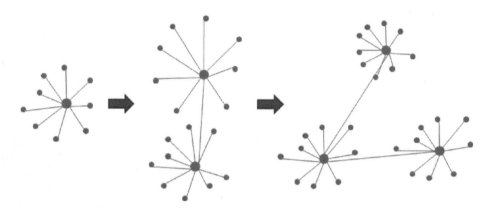

Figure 1-5. *Client/server model in more and more decentralized mode*

In Figure 1-6, observe how peer-to-peer networks work when there is no central server.

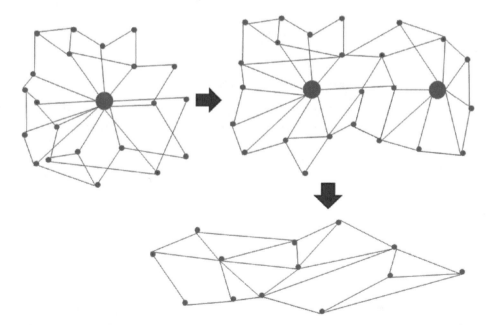

Figure 1-6. *Peer-to-peer model in more and more decentralized mode*

OK, now that you are convinced about why we need DLT, let's also discuss the benefits of Blockchain and how Blockchain is different from and similar to DLT.

Benefits of Blockchain

One may wonder if Blockchain is another type of database and why we created it in the first place. Please note that Blockchain was introduced to us through Bitcoin, a cryptocurrency, and it was conceptualized to address the needs of digital currency in a way that a traditional database cannot.

- The data in a Blockchain ledger can't be altered.

- It's a highly secured database that uses public and private keys for transactions.

- The database is publicly available for everyone to validate and add transactions.

- Being decentralized, there is no downtime in Blockchain and hence transactions can be added anytime and from anywhere.

- It could be public or private as per the individual's or organization's business needs and hence is flexible.

- Ledger is open to auditing anytime.

DLT vs. Blockchain

Blockchain is a special use case of DLT. Once you explore more on Blockchain, come back to this section and read it again to figure out where they are similar and where they differ.

Similarities

- Both use public/private-key cryptography

- Both use hashing

- Both use peer-to-peer model for communication

Differences

- Blockchain uses native currency, which is a mandate; DLT does not

- Blockchain is distributed (i.e., all data can be visible to all nodes); DLT is not

- Blockchain is permission-less; DLT is not

- Blockchain works with PoW (though soon Ethereum will be coming out with Proof of Stake [PoS]); DLT does not

Blockchain Business Value

The year 2018 was a massive year for Blockchain. From Proof of Concepts (PoCs) to pilots, slowly and yet steadily organizations started advancing their Blockchain journey toward production. Oracle sees 10% of global GDP stored in Blockchain by 2027, and Deloitte predicts that by 2025, ~10% of global GDP will be stored in Blockchain. As per the research institute IDC, worldwide Blockchain spending will grow 81.2% to $9.7 billion in 2021. Many organizations and corporations are paying double the standard salary to professionals who are hands on with Blockchain technology, and the trend is just beginning. Reports say that in many countries, including India, only 1 in 400 IT professionals are hands on with the technology, which leaves huge room for training and placement.

Blockchain Internals

Now let's see how data is added to a Blockchain ledger. Consider a book, as represented in Figure 1-7, that has 100 pages, with a page number at the top of each page. If one page is torn out from the book, the reader would easily trace it out. The same is true for a Blockchain store.

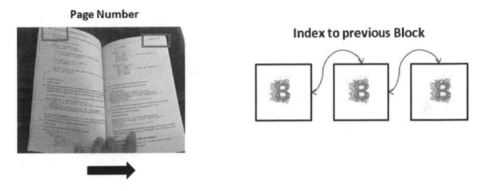

Figure 1-7. *Indexing in Blockchain*

Blockchain Transaction and Blocks

As the name suggests, Blockchain is a chain of blocks where each block points to a previous block.

Each block consists of

- A block header

- One or more transactions in the block

If we compare Blockchain data store to a book, then each block represents a page in the book and transactions quoted in the individual block are synonymous to lines on a page in the book.

The first block in a Blockchain ledger as shown in Figure 1-8 is known as a genesis block. Umers or uncle blocks are the detached blocks not chosen for inclusion in the consensus Blockchain. However, miners (to be explained validators of transaction) can also discover smaller numbers of tokens.

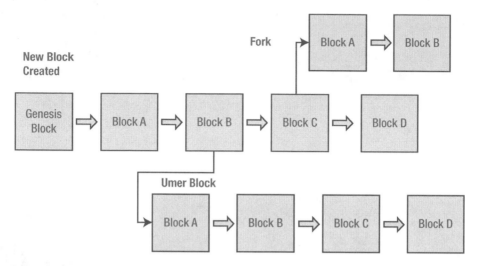

Figure 1-8. *How Blockchain progresses*

Different Types of Blocks

Genesis Blocks: The first block in a Blockchain network is known as a genesis block.

Orphan Blocks: Orphan blocks (often referred to in Bitcoin) are valid blocks that are nonetheless rejected by the network. Orphan blocks occur when two miners produce a block at similar times, but due to latency issues, one is chosen over another. This leads to a fork in the Blockchain.

Stale Blocks: When one miner is successful in mining a block, then other miners working on their versions of a similar block become old or stale.

Umer Blocks: Umer or uncle blocks are validated blocks often associated with Ethereum and are similar to orphan blocks in Bitcoin. They are rejected by the network due to formation of another longer fork. However, unlike orphan blocks, the miner in an Ethereum network gets some reward, which is less than for normal blocks.

Block Header

A Blockchain is made up of a series of blocks that are joined together with a special logic. Every block has a block header, which has the following information, also shown in Figure 1-9.

- Hash of previous block

- Timestamp

- Mining or difficulty level

- A PoW nonce

- A root hash for the Merkle tree containing the transactions for that block

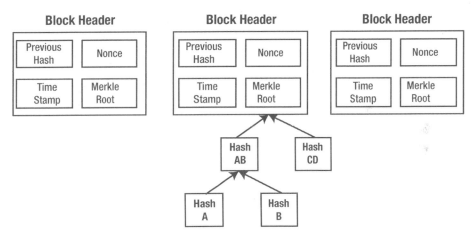

Figure 1-9. Blocks in Blockchain

Merkle Tree

As per Wikipedia, "In cryptography and computer science, a hash tree or Merkle tree is a tree in which every leaf node is labeled with the hash of a data block and every nonleaf node is labeled with the cryptographic hash of the labels of its child nodes."

Well, what does that mean? A Merkle tree represents data in its nascent form as well as in its hashed value. At the bottom of the tree, you can see real values called leaf nodes.

As shown in Figure 1-10, let's say in the Blockchain we have three blocks. In the middle block B, there are eight transactions T(A) to T(H). Now let's see how the Merkle tree is formed.

All of these transactions are first converted to their hash values: H(A) to H(H).

Then, each hash value is paired with another hash value next to it to create a new hash value: H(A) + H(B) = H(AB). What if we have an odd number of transactions, for example, H(G) as the last hash? Then it creates a hash with itself, that is, H(GG).

This process continues till we reach a single hash of all the transactions of the current block, that is, H(ABCDEFGH). This is called the Merkle root.

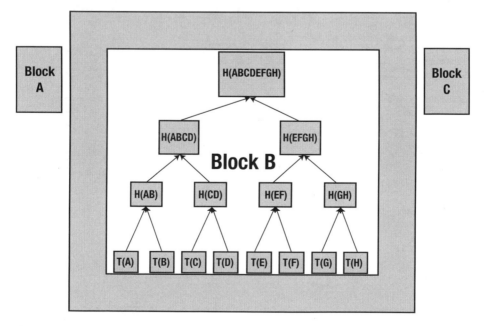

Figure 1-10. *Merkle tree*

Now this Merkle root goes to the block header and also to the next block, where it gets saved as the hash of previous block.

"Merkle trees are a fundamental part of what makes Blockchains tick. Although it is definitely theoretically possible to make a Blockchain without Merkle trees, simply by creating giant block headers that directly contain every transaction, doing so poses large scalability challenges that arguably put the ability to trustlessly use Blockchains out of the reach of all but the most powerful computers in the long term."

The preceding lines are by Ethereum cofounder Vitalik Buterin. They help in maintaining the sanity and integrity of the entire Blockchain. If any transaction data in the Blockchain gets altered, then the hash value would alter and ultimately the Merkle root would alter and would mismatch with the original Merkle root saved in the next block; hence the Blockchain would get invalidated. This is the magic formula by which data remains tamperproof and secure online in a public Blockchain as Bitcoin or Ethereum.

Dealing with Double Spending

Double spending is an issue in the Blockchain ecosystem, and different Blockchain and DLT networks handle it using different algorithms. Let's say Party A, which has $100, has to pay $100 to Party B and $100 to Party C. In the real world, this is not possible as payment would be in physical currency. But in the digital world, especially in the Blockchain ecosystem, if Party A in quick succession creates two transactions to Parties B and C each with $100 before the earlier one is confirmed, then it's possible that both transactions would be executed independently. This issue is called double spending. In Figure 1-11, you can see how transactions are tracked in consecutive blocks.

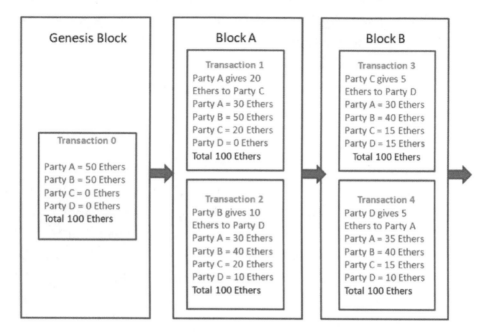

Figure 1-11. *Tracking of transactions in Blockchain*

In a Blockchain network, such issues are prevented by tracing each transaction closely. When the genesis block is added, the network is assigned a finite supply of cryptocurrency and then those currencies are exchanged between parties as the transactions go on. Each time a block is added, miners thoroughly calculate if the entire supply remains the same and no data has been tampered with. Thus, double spending is completely avoided.

Blockchain Hashing

Hashing is an algorithm that takes any string as input and gives us another string as output that has a fixed length. It's nearly impossible to decipher the input from the output string. Also, it does not matter how many times or at whatever time interval you hash the input string; the output string would always remain the same. Furthermore, the length of output string would always remain the same for different inputs big or small; only the output contents would be different. There are different industry standard hashing algorithms available in the market: SHA-1, SHA-2, SHA-256, and so on. Hashing is very frequently used for comparing secure data. For example, passwords are most often not stored in databases in nascent form; rather their hashed value is stored and whenever the user logs in again, the hash value of supplied password is crosschecked with the saved hash value to authenticate the user.

So what's the need for hashing in Blockchain? As already discussed, in Blockchain we calculate hash values of data and then create a hash of all hashes of transactions and store it in the header of each block. Also, each block has a hash value similar to that of the preceding block. This makes the entire Blockchain bound together with a complex logic. Hence, it is extremely difficult for any attacker to decipher the whole dataset and malignly access the data.

Public and Private Keys

When someone sends you crypto coins over the Blockchain, they actually send them to a hashed version of what's known as the "public key." There is another key that is hidden from them; this is known as the "private key." This private key is used to derive the public key. Everyone in the Blockchain network knows their own private key. It's like a master key to your locker in a bank and should not be shared with anyone, unless you want your cryptocurrencies to be stolen!

As shown in Figure 1-12, the private key is used to mathematically derive the public key, which is then transformed with a hash function to produce the address, which other people can see. You receive cryptocurrencies that others send to your address.

Figure 1-12. *Public and private keys*

At this point, you may be asking yourself, if a public key is derived from a private key, couldn't someone create a reverse key generator that derives private keys from public keys, allowing them to steal anyone's coins in the process? Cryptocurrencies solve this issue by using a complicated mathematical algorithm to generate the public keys: as shown in Figure 1-13, the algorithm makes it very easy to generate public keys from private keys, but it is very difficult to "reverse" the algorithm to accomplish the opposite.

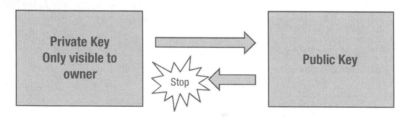

Figure 1-13. *Private key cannot be extracted from public key*

How Bitcoin Works

Now let's connect the dots and find out how Bitcoin or a public Blockchain works in a broad way.

- Bitcoins are stored in digital wallets. Each user has a wallet that has a public and private key. The public key is also called the address or account of the user. The private key is like the password.

- Once two parties/users set up their wallets, they can exchange Bitcoins in the network.

When Party A pays x number of Bitcoins to Party B as shown in Figure 1-14, they have to create the hashed value of the transaction and encrypt using their private key. The transaction then gets broadcast over the network both in raw form and in hashed + encrypted form.

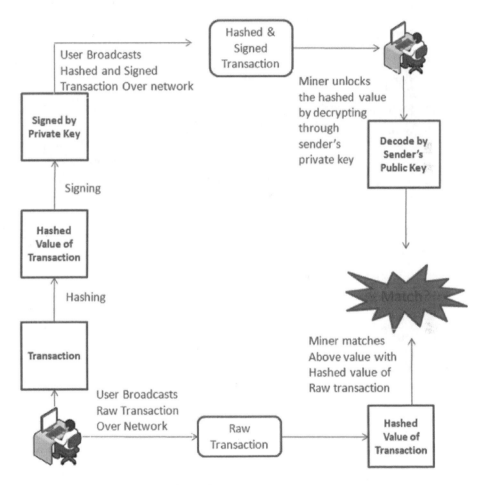

Figure 1-14. *Bitcoin order of execution*

- Miners or validators decrypt the hashed value of the transaction by using the public key of the owner and then match the hashed value of the raw transaction with this value. In such a way, the nonrepudiation as well as the integrity of the data is verified.

- Now miners verify and add validated transactions to their version of blocks.

- If a miner finishes validation and PoW (a mathematical puzzle) faster than others, they publish a new block with new transactions to the network.

- Other users validate the new block and add it to their version of Blockchain. If 51% or more users validate (in consensus) and add the block, then it gets added to the Blockchain.

- In the entire process, the miner who solved the puzzle and added transactions to the new block publishing it would be rewarded by a few Bitcoins. Currently this bounty is 12.5 Bitcoins; this value will halve every 210,000 blocks.

- The entire procedure happens within 10 minutes. If the block not validated within this time, it becomes an orphan block.

The network is helped by the hashing process as well as the public/private-key pair for making the entire network trustworthy even with untrusted nodes. When a party sends Bitcoins to another party, then the transaction is hashed and signed with the sender's private key for confirmation of origin. The same data is also broadcast in raw form. The validators know that the transaction is an authorized one by its signature.

Anyone can unlock and read the hashed version using the sender's public key. Also, as the same data is broadcast in raw form, the validator can use the same hash function and match it with the hashed data after unencryption to check nonrepudiation.

Transactions

Transactions are the most interesting part of the Bitcoin network, which the validators check and add to their version of blocks. Each transaction must have one or more inputs and outputs. Output of one transaction would go as input to another transaction. Outputs of all transactions included in Blockchain can be categorized as either unspent transaction outputs (UTXOs) or spent transaction outputs. An output is considered unspent when it's not yet been used as an input to a new transaction. Double spending is prohibited by validators by checking the inputs and outputs of these transactions. Each output of a particular transaction can only be spent once. For a payment to be valid, it must only use UTXOs as inputs.

In a public Blockchain network like Bitcoin, there could be changes in consensus rules at multiple times, and at any point of time there could be nodes that update themselves with a new set of rules or stay with the previous version. This is figured out with a version number, which informs Bitcoin users which set of consensus rules to use to validate it. If a transaction's output exceeds its inputs, the transaction will be rejected. However, if the inputs exceed the value of the outputs, any difference in value may be claimed as a transaction fee by the Bitcoin miner who creates the block containing that transaction. It's the validator's job to check all of it.

Possible Attacks on Bitcoin Network

Bitcoin and its inherent Blockchain technology are not completely foolproof. It's based on the assumption that most of the users in the network are honest and any dishonest user would be discarded from the system, which is not always true.

Double Spending

Double spending is spending the same money twice. In the physical world with fiat cash, this might be difficult, but in the digital world it is possible. In banking transactions, if there is double spending then the centralized server would discard it. In interbank transfers, the central bank checks each transaction, verifies the validity of accounts and the amounts in them, and then allows the transfer. If there is any issue, transactions are reverted in banks. Also, there is Know Your Customer (KYC) verification as added security for background verification of each person on the network.

However, since Bitcoin is a decentralized system, how can double spending be avoided?

- In a Bitcoin Blockchain network, all users can see unspent or available Satoshis in each user account.

- When a new transaction is broadcast, miners validate each transaction on the basis of the current status of the respective accounts, along with the available Satoshis in them, and check inputs and outputs of each transaction.

- If there is an attempt to spend the same Satoshis more than once, transactions can come to miners during formation of one block or separate blocks.

- If transactions are part of same block, then miners accept only the first transaction and invalidate the others.

- If transactions are part of separate blocks, the first one gets accepted and the block gets added to the Blockchain, so miners working on the next block see Satoshis getting subtracted from the account and hence discard the second transaction.

- In case any miner adds the second transaction to a second block by mistake, completes the PoW fastest, and broadcasts it, other miners would invalidate that block.

Double spending in Blockchain mostly happens in two different ways:

- *Race Condition:* If you send two transactions in quick succession it sometimes creates confusion among the miners, but soon other users sort this out. The block that quickly gathers more blocks to form "Longest Chain" is finally joined by others and considered valid; the other one is rejected.

- *51% Attack:* The malicious node acquires more than 51% hash power of the network, and together these hash powers validate erroneous transactions and add respective blocks to the Blockchain, which are validated by other nodes that work in a group. This is theoretically possible. Yet it would be too expensive and may require more investment than the transactions themselves.

DDoS Attack

Distributed denial of service (DDoS) attacks are not confined to Bitcoin or public Blockchain networks. In DDoS, the attacker sends a huge number of requests to overwhelm servers.

A PoW system (or protocol, or function) is an economical measure to deter denial of service attacks and other service abuses such as spam on a network by requiring some work from the service requester, usually meaning processing time by a computer.

Using PoW, such attacks can be deterred to a great extent, and yet such attacks are still possible. The logic is that someone would probably not waste a lot of computational power for altering a transaction whose worth might be much less than the hash power wasted.

Sybil or 51% Attack

A Sybil attack is an attack where a single adversary is controlling multiple nodes on a network. It is unknown to the network that the nodes are controlled by the same adversarial entity. The reputation system is subverted by forging identities in peer-to-peer networks.

A 51% attack is a type of Sybil attack. If an attacker succeeds in filling the network with 51% or more clients, then they can control the decisions in the Bitcoin network.

Owning so many nodes is costly, and yet pool miners can do this if a particular pool has more than 50% hashing power of the entire network. That's the reason many public Blockchain networks are moving away from a voting mechanism (PoW) and opting for other consensus rules.

Eclipse Attack

As the name suggests, an eclipse attack kind of blinds a node and disconnects it, preventing a cryptocurrency user from connecting to real peers. The victim node hence would not get updated with latest data.

Like a Sybil attack, it's also an attack on the network; however, contrary to a Sybil attack, which is on the whole of the network, this attack is on individual node basis.

Also, it's interesting to note that a Sybil attack is what an adversary uses in order to perform an eclipse attack. This is because a Bitcoin node normally connects to multiple peers. The adversary therefore would have to impersonate all peers of the victim in order to eclipse the victim from the rest of the network.

MitM Attack

A Man in the Middle (MitM) attack is one in which an attacker places himself between two peer nodes in the network. They redirect victims' funds to their own wallets by changing the destination address of cryptocurrency transactions.

In the case of the ledger wallet, a malware installed on the target computer changes the destination address of Bitcoin transactions and replaces it with the address of the attacker's wallet.

The only way users can detect and stop the attack is to manually compare the address displayed on their computer with the one that appears on the ledger's display.

Consensus

We already know Blockchain is a distributed decentralized ledger where data is saved with common consensus between all the parties. Consensus is never an issue with a traditional centralized database or ledger, as it has a single owner or a central authority responsible for taking all the decisions, along with validating and storing the data. However, Blockchain is a public ledger that deals with multiple peers. So how can all the participants agree on the current state of the Blockchain and reach a common consensus to store data when they do not trust each other? Different Blockchain and DLT frameworks have worked on this puzzle and have come up with different solutions. Broadly, the consensus mechanisms can be mainly divided into the following types:

- Proof of Work (PoW)

- Proof of Stake (PoS)

- Delegated Proof of Stake (DPoS)

- Proof of Authority (PoA)

- Practical Byzantine Fault Tolerance (PBFT)

- Directed Acyclic Graphs (DAGs)

Currently, these consensus mechanisms are widely adopted by different Blockchain and DLT frameworks. A particular model can be chosen over others as per an organization's business demands. Performance, scalability, and security are major factors before finalizing any one of them over others.

PoW

PoW was the first consensus mechanism introduced with Bitcoin. In PoW, all the miners (discussed in the next section) compete to solve a mathematical problem, and the one who solves it fastest becomes the winner. Soon, other miners start validating it till it reaches a preagreed percentage voting (51% or 90% as per configuration). PoW works on the "longest chain" rule: that is, if there are forks created due to different miners agreeing to different side chains, then the longest chain that moves the fastest is the most trustworthy and soon others would start following that chain and other side chains would be discarded.

Used By: Bitcoin, Ethereum

Advantages: Time tested, safe

Disadvantages: Too slow, massive power consumption

Mining

The process of validating transactions and adding a block to the Blockchain network is called mining. The participant users who mine are called miners. But why would someone like to do that? It's because the miners are rewarded with a fraction of cryptocurrency that fuels the Blockchain framework.

PoS

PoS consensus has nothing to do with mining, yet it still validates the blocks and adds to Blockchain. This collateral-based consensus algorithm depends on the validator's economic stake in the network: that is, each validator must own some stake in the network by depositing some money into the network. In PoS-based consensus for public Blockchains, a set of validators take turns proposing and voting on the next block, and the weight of each validator's vote depends on the size of its deposit.

Used By: Ethereum's upcoming Casper model of consensus

Advantages: Security, reduced risk of centralization, and energy efficiency

Disadvantages: In a way, PoS is more prone to attack, as there is no computational factor as in PoW to keep the network safe

Minting

Here in PoS, the entire process of validating a new block and getting a fraction of the cryptocurrency as a reward is called minting (not mining).

DPoS

The delegated PoS (DPoS) is a variation of the PoS consensus model in which all the users vote to select the ones who would be the final approvers of transactions in a democratic way.

Used By: EOS, Bitshares

Advantages: Superfast, scalable, and high energy efficiency

Disadvantages: None

PoA

PoA is a modified version of PoS where identity is at stake instead of monetary value. In this consensus model, transactions and blocks are validated by approved accounts, known as validators. An individual gets the right to be an approving authority only after producing their valid identity proof. Hence, there is no need for mining.

Used By: Ethereum's Parity supports PoA consensus model

Advantages: Security, no mining, high in scalability and performance

Disadvantages: None

PBFT

The PBFT model of consensus is derived from a classic problem of wars in ancient times. Let's say several Byzantine generals with their respective army groups have surrounded an enemy fort. In order to conquer the fort, it's crucial that most of the generals must attack the fort at the same time and work in unity. However, whether they would attack the fort and at what time would be a collective decision among all of them, which they would reach by sharing data between each other. Let's say General 1 sends a message to Generals 2, 3, and 4 to attack at 4:30 p.m., and all send their acknowledgement to the proposal as "Yes." However, it's possible that one of them is a traitor and would actually not oblige when common attack is required. Consensus in such a system, which is equivalent to a win in the war, is achieved if a minimum particular threshold is achieved; that is, let's say 2/3 of all generals actually are loyal and work in unison.

Used By: Hyperledger, Ripple, Stellar

Advantages: High transaction throughput

Disadvantages: Centralized/permissioned

DAGs

DAGs are a form of consensus that doesn't use the Blockchain data structure and handles transactions mostly asynchronously. Tangle is the DAG consensus algorithm used by IOTA. In order to send an IOTA transaction, you need to validate two previous transactions you're received.

Used By: IOTA, HashGraph, Nano

Advantages: Infinitely scalable, speed increases as network grows, best suited for microtransactions

Disadvantages: Works well only with high amount of traffic; without traffic may have initiation problem

Fork in Blockchain

If you start working with a Blockchain framework such as Ethereum, you will often come across forks. Forks in Blockchain are of two types:

- Soft fork

- Hard fork

Soft Fork

While transactions are added to a block and the block gets validated by any consensus model (e.g., PoW or PoA), a temporary fork might get created either accidentally or otherwise, as people may have different versions of the same Blockchain ledger. In most cases, they are sorted out soon, as most people on network start accepting the longest chain most valid. The side chains are discarded and acknowledged as faulty blocks. They are called soft forks.

Soft forks have vulnerability for being exposed to denial of service attacks, which may prevent the network from processing valid transactions at negligible expense to the attacker. Just as in other DoS attacks, an attacker can flood the network with transactions that have high computation complexity, and end by performing an operation on the Decentralized Autonomous Organization (DAO) contract. Hence, one has to be careful with soft fork.

Hard Fork

Hard forks are needed from time to time, as software has to pass through changes or version upgrades. As shown in Figure 1-15, in such processes two different versions of the Blockchain are created sharing the same origin; this is often called a hard fork. Depending upon the rule that denotes intensity of change to the original version, the fork is labeled as a soft fork or a hard fork. The primary difference between a soft and a hard fork is that soft forks are backward compatible whereas hard forks are not.

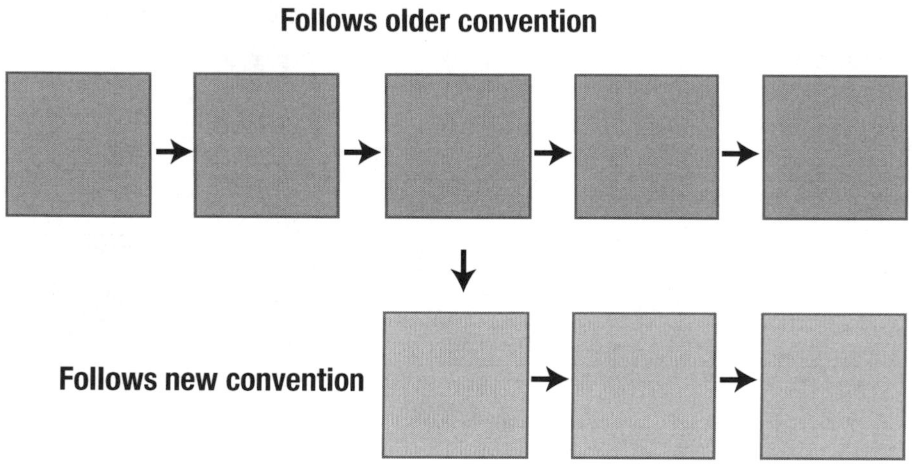

Follows older convention

Follows new convention

Figure 1-15. Fork in Blockchain

Bitcoin, whose genesis or first block was created back in 2009, has undergone many hard forks since then. Some of them are named as follows:

- Bitcoin XT

- Bitcoin Classic

- Bitcoin Unlimited

- Segregated Witness

- Bitcoin Cash

- Bitcoin Gold

- SegWit2X

Types of Visibilities in Blockchain Networks

Blockchain networks are of different visibilities (i.e., public, private, permissioned, consortium, etc.) that suit different business needs.

Public Blockchain

Blockchain is completely transparent and publicly accessible (most likely on the Internet), and transactions are open to all on the network. They need volunteers or miners to validate and secure entries, through PoW, PoS, or any other consensus method. Bitcoin is a perfect example of a public Blockchain network. Even Ethereum in its nascent form is a public Blockchain network.

Advantages: No infrastructure costs; no need to maintain servers or system administrators, which radically reduces the costs of creating and running decentralized applications (dApps)

Private Blockchain

In private Blockchain, all permissions are kept centralized to an organization, and hence what it has is a partial feature list of Blockchain; it's rather just a distributed database. It allows an organization with compliance and privacy requirements to implement Blockchain.

Monax and MultiChain are fine examples of private Blockchains. Ethereum can be configured to work on a private Blockchain network. In fact, many people nowadays prefer private Blockchains, as they do not wish to expose their data to the entire world through a public network.

Advantages: Scales well, faster execution, no token needed to procure for mining

Consortium or Federated Blockchain

Consortium Blockchain is partly private. Instead of allowing any person with an Internet connection to participate in the verification of transaction processes or allowing only one company to have full control, a few selected nodes are predetermined. For example, in a trade finance use case, the consortium may consist of participating banks, importers, exporters, ports of sending and receiving countries, customs officials, and so on. Some of these participants will have write access and some or all will have read access.

It is not fully decentralized like public Blockchain.

Quorum, R3 Corda, Hyperledger Fabric, and so on are based on this principle. Like the private Blockchain, they are fast, efficient, and secure.

Be it a fully decentralized public Blockchain or a fully private Blockchain or even a consortium Blockchain, all have potential use cases and there could be a Blockchain solution that is a permutation of more than one. We have to study our business use case well and choose the one that suits us the best.

Hybrid Blockchain

Many use cases do not fit into any of the preceding requirements for public or private Blockchain; rather, they might need a solution which is a combination of multiple Blockchains. Hybrid Blockchain is one such solution that offers the benefits of both public and private Blockchain. There are many different hybrid approaches in Blockchain; however, mostly they have a public Blockchain where anyone can join and participate in the transaction. There could also be a private Blockchain associated with a public one where only a well-known and invited centralized body can join. In such hybrid networks, we can have multiple consensus mechanisms like PoW and PoS. PoW miners from a public network still create blocks with valid transactions. However, only selected PoS miners from a private network can vote and add the block to the public Blockchain for everyone to get access to the data. This eliminates the 51% attack risks.

There are quite a few organizations wishing to adopt this approach in the future, Xinfin being one of the leaders in hybrid Blockchain. Ripple is also heading toward a hybrid approach and recommends the same for the banks.

Ethereum, the First Player

After Ethereum, many other Blockchain as well as DLT frameworks have flooded the market; I have jotted down a few in the "Leading Blockchain and DLT Protocols" section. However, Ethereum is still the Blockchain haven for many. Here are few reasons:

- Ethereum has been in market since July 2015; it's the time-tested oldest player here.

- You can find a huge development network with Ethereum.

- There are plenty of tools and frameworks built on top of Ethereum; for example, Quorum, Truffle, MetaMask, Embark.

- There are enough developers available in the market with Ethereum skill sets.

- Most major Cloud enablers, such as Amazon Web Service, Azure, Google Cloud, and so on, have either started providing Ethereum templates as part of the service or are planning to do so.

- Ethereum is open source.

Limitations of Ethereum

There is no disadvantage of Ethereum as such; yet being a public Blockchain, it comes with a certain number of limitations:

- Public Blockchains are not suitable for all.

- At the time of writing, Ethereum is slow. It takes 12+ seconds for miners to validate and add a block to an Ethereum Blockchain network.

Ethereum is not the first choice to work as a private permissioned distributed ledger. A lot of extra work is needed to set up that kind of capability in Ethereum. We can rather choose from a number of private permissioned DLTs available in the market. I will now discuss some of them briefly.

Leading Blockchain and DLT Protocols

There are many Blockchain and DLT frameworks available in the market today. However, let's discuss some of the most popular. If you wish to know more you may refer to my other book, *BlockChain: From Concept to Execution* (BPB Publications, 2018), which details most of them.

Quorum

Quorum is the Enterprise-focused version of Ethereum. Quorum addresses specific challenges to Blockchain technology adoption within the financial industry and beyond. Quorum has developed capabilities to address requirements of many industries and verticals.

Ripple

Ripple claims it's "the world's only enterprise Blockchain solution for global payments." Unlike many other cryptocurrencies, Ripple is centralized, and it comes with a finite supply of currencies. Also, it claims to be the most scalable Blockchain solution on the market.

Hyperledger Fabric

Hyperledger Fabric is one of the many projects running under the Hyperledger umbrella. Originally contributed by IBM, today it is the most widely used private permissioned framework on the market. While Ethereum has been running on production for the past few years, Hyperledger Fabric is still maturing. The July 2017 released version is claimed to be production ready. In many ways, the architecture and features of Hyperledger Fabric are pretty similar to those of R3 Corda, as they are built on similar specifications.

R3 Corda

R3 (R3CEV LLC) is a distributed database technology company that leads a consortium of more than 200 of the world's biggest banks and financial institutions in research and development of Blockchain database usage in the financial system.

R3 Corda is a joint venture that started in September 2015 between R3 and numerous banks and financial groups to create a framework that is more than a traditional Blockchain. Corda is especially crafted to suit the need of financial institutes such as speed, privacy, scalability, security, and so on. In fact, Corda is simply a DLT and not a Blockchain in terms of its architecture. However, it comes with all the advantages that Blockchain offers: distribution, decentralization, fraudproof, append-only, secure, and so on.

Initially, Corda was proposed as a DLT framework primarily crafted for financial use cases; today it has emerged as the DLT leader in the insurance space. Swiss Re, MetLife, EY, Maersk, EY, AIG, AON, Marine Insurance, Cognizant, and Capgemini are a few names currently trying Corda for their insurance products. As per recent news from Corda, 39 firms completed a global trial of KYC on Corda Blockchain platform, and many banks have built real-time international payments solutions on the Corda DLT platform.

MultiChain

MultiChain is another very promising private permissioned Blockchain framework made up of Bitcoin fork. It's open source and well documented, and it comes with a low learning curve and fast deployment.

Symbiont

Founded in 2015, Symbiont is a Blockchain technology company based in New York City, developing products in smart contracts and distributed ledgers for use in capital markets.

OpenChain

OpenChain is an open source, Enterprise-ready Blockchain technology platform most suitable for organizations wishing to issue and manage digital assets in a robust, secure, and scalable way.

Cardano

Launched in September 2017 by Blockchain Development Output Hong Kong (IOHK), Cardano is a decentralized Blockchain platform on open source smart contracts that works on a PoS algorithm and provides a base for the cryptocurrency ADA. Its first version was released in September 2017.

IOTA

IOTA is a distributed ledger protocol just like Ethereum, yet it comes with a revolutionary new architecture called "Tangle." With feeless micropayments, it will enable communication between connected devices, leading to a novel "machine economy" for which IOTA boasts of being the backbone of IoT.

EOS

Based on a white paper released in 2017, EOS is another latest player in the open source Blockchain market. It's a Blockchain-based, decentralized operating system designed to support commercial-scale decentralized applications by providing all of the necessary core functionality including databases, accounts with permissions, scheduling, authentication, handling communication between the application and the Internet, and so on, thus allowing developers to focus on their own particular business logic. Loaded with features, it's often termed as the "Ethereum Killer" and "Ethereum with a motor."

HashGraph

The Hedera HashGraph platform is less constrained than Blockchain and provides a new form of distributed consensus. It caters to the same group of people who don't know or trust each other to securely collaborate and transact online without the need for a trusted intermediary. The advantages of this platform over Blockchain are that it's lightning fast, secure, and fair, and doesn't require compute-intensive PoW. As per some experts, Hedera HashGraph is pretty much likely to replace Blockchain altogether.

Quiz

1. Blockchain is

    A. A private ledger

    B. A public ledger

    C. An immutable, append-only ledger

    D. All of the above

2. A Blockchain ledger is always associated with a cryptocurrency

    A. True

    B. False

3. What are the current issues with public Blockchain?

    A. Scalability

    B. Response time

    C. Forking

    D. All of the above

4. Are all cryptocurrencies decentralized?

    A. Yes, it's a mandate

    B. No, there are some cryptocurrencies that have centralized architecture

5. Which of the following protocols does not have a traditional Blockchain architecture?

    A. Bitcoin

    B. Ethereum

    C. MultiChain

    D. Corda

Answers

1 D, 2 B, 3 D, 4 B, 5 D

Reference

Ethereum for Architects and Developers by Debajani Mohanty (Apress, 2019)

CHAPTER 2

Corda Architecture

In this chapter, we are going to cover the building blocks of Corda such as its network service for managing the registration process of nodes, Corda ledger with its identity services, and further details on business flows, data states, transactions, smart contracts, and so on.

If you are coming from an Ethereum or Hyperledger Fabric background, the architecture of Corda will surprise you, as many concepts of Corda are inherently unique and different from most of its parallel technologies; this has helped Corda to gather so many esteemed clients in such a small time span. Here are a few key concepts.

The Doorman, Network Service

The way R3 Corda works is pretty different from traditional Blockchain networks. In public Blockchain networks such as Bitcoin or Ethereum, anyone can join the Blockchain network and will be identified only by a pseudonymous public address. Also, messages are transmitted in a raw form to the network. This architecture might not be suitable to enterprises where security and privacy of messages are paramount. In the Corda network, each node is a verified IP address that is agreed between business counterparties before finalizing a contract. These IP addresses representing different organizations go through a stringent KYC process

© Debajani Mohanty 2019
D. Mohanty, *R3 Corda for Architects and Developers*,
https://doi.org/10.1007/978-1-4842-4529-3_2

and are added to the network through a network map service called "the doorman." All nodes can use this network map service to transact with other nodes in a peer-to-peer fashion.

Unlike public Blockchain networks such as Bitcoin and Ethereum, where broadcasting or gossip networks are in use, in Corda, nodes communicate on a peer-to-peer basis with Transport Layer Security (TLS)-encrypted messages sent over AMQP/1.0.

The Corda Ledger

In Corda, when nodes wish to do a business transaction with each other, the data is stored in their individual databases or ledgers after contractual validation and verification by notary. There can be many notary nodes on a Corda network, and hence it's not a single point of failure. The nodes that are not related to the transaction are unable to have access to this data.

Identity

Identity in Corda is related to the identity of nodes that actually stand for the individual organizations that participate in the DLT network. Hence each node comes with its own legal name, IP address, and X.509 certificate signed by the doorman. Identity in the Corda network may represent an organization or a service assisting the DLT network.

State

In Corda, data is maintained by state objects. Data state is immutable; however, state can change with each transaction and we can always check the previous state of data for traceability. Each node maintains a local database called "vault" that maintains current data (also known as unconsumed state) as well as previous data (called consumed state) with timestamps. Each vault has many different versions of data in the form of state objects, out of which only one is current and the rest are historic data.

Contracts

In Corda, every transaction to be executed has to be signed by each of the concerned nodes' notaries and also has to be contractually valid.

There is a one-to-one relationship between a contract and a state.

Smart contracts in Corda can be written in JVM languages as Kotlin or Java. Though the inherent APIs of Corda are written in Kotlin, more and more developers nowadays are writing this part in Java for its wide acceptance as a coding language.

Ricardian Contract

Ricardian contracts, invented by Ian Grigg in 1996, empower legal contracts to be translated to digital counterparts with the original legal prose remaining intact. This approach allows a contract to move from the paper-based documents of law to a world of cryptography and into the world of accountancy. In Corda, smart contracts are allowed to contain legal prose, called smart legal contracts (referring to Ricardian contracts). We will explore more in chapter 3 as we learn how to write a contract in Corda.

Transaction

Corda defines a transaction as "a proposal to update the ledger" that will be committed if contractually valid, that is, signed by all relevant parties and notary. Last but not least, it should have no double spends.

Corda uses a UTXO (unspent transaction output) model where a transaction can have from zero to many inputs and outputs.

Transaction inputs can be any of the following:

- Command

- Attachment

- Timestamp

Flow

Flow is a sequence of steps that tells a node how to achieve a specific ledger update. Flow involves contract validations as well as state updates.

Consensus

In Corda, only related parties as well as notaries participate in the transaction, and hence there is no need of consensus from other nodes like most of the Blockchain platforms. The concerned parties check the programmed contractual validity and the uniqueness of the transaction.

Notary

A notary is a special node that gets involved in transactions, validating them and preventing double spends. A Corda network can have many notaries with different responsibilities as follows:

- Privacy – Corda can have multiple validating and nonvalidating notary services on the same network working with independent algorithms. Programmatically, a node can choose a notary on a per-transaction basis.

- Load balancing – We can also distribute transaction load over multiple notaries, which allows higher transaction throughput for the platform overall.

- Low latency – A notary physically closer to the transacting parties can be chosen over others to minimize latency.

Time Window

Timestamping is an integral part of contractual validation, as most real-life smart contracts often have a time window for an activity of payment. If a transaction happens after that time period, the contract should invalidate it. We will check programmatically how to handle this in chapter 4, where we cover a sample code for a land registry.

Oracles

Applications deployed on DLT as Corda are deployed in a private permissioned network totally cut off from external network. But what if there is a need to get connected to some external service for retrieving data like location details, exchange rate, and so on? For that, we use Oracle services.

GDPR, the Blockchain Killer!

It's a general practice for most of us who create our accounts on social media such as LinkedIn, Facebook, Twitter, Instagram, and so on to leave personal data footprints on these websites. How many of us ever wondered if these platforms offer us a solution to erase all this personal information from their storage as and when needed? Perhaps because of the Facebook data breach scandal, many individuals as well as organizations have started reviewing their policies on such matters of data security. Nonetheless, information available on such websites without adequate controls in place always helps criminals and hackers to achieve their goals. It's no surprise that demand for cybersecurity professionals is ever on the rise, as data protection is a major challenge for every industry today.

Some of the data regulations that most of us might have come across are as follows:

- Payment Card Industry Data Security Standard (PCI- DSS)

- Health Insurance Portability and Accountability Act (HIPAA)

- The Sarbanes-Oxley Act

- Federal Information Security Management Act of 2002 (FISMA)

- Gramm-Leach-Bliley Act (GLBA)

- Family Educational Rights and Privacy Act (FERPA)

The newest one added to the list is the General Data Protection Regulation (`https://gdpr-info.eu/`), widely known as GDPR. This is a regulation in EU law on data protection and privacy for citizens within the European Union. The goal of this act, which has been enforced since 25 May 2018, is to assign the following rights to consumers:

- The right to access information related to you

- The right to be forgotten

- The right to data portability

- The right to make companies edit and correct information about you

- The right to control usage of personal data within geographic boundaries.

As per the newly devised law, violation of the GDPR protocol may lead to a penalty of "up to €20 million, or 4% of the worldwide annual revenue of the prior financial year, whichever is higher" (`www.gdpreu.org/compliance/fines-and-penalties/`). Hence, noncompliance with this act might negatively affect many businesses if they are not prepared for the implications of the newly devised rules on data. Also, following the EU, many other countries and regions may come up with their own versions of such data protection laws.

The GDPR data reformation journey initiated in January 2012, when not many were aware of a next-generation Big Bang named "Blockchain." Hence, many of the data protection needs are in some way incompatible with those of Blockchain, especially when it's implemented in the public domain.

Now let's see how GDPR would affect Blockchain, where data is mostly public and shared among all the participating nodes.

- Data in public Blockchain as Bitcoin, Ethereum, and so on is universal. Hence there is little control applicable to this decentralized system to enforce a rule prohibiting data from crossing a geographic boundary.

- One of the GDPR regulations requires provision for deletion of personal data on a need basis. However, in traditional Blockchain, this is not possible as erasing any historical data from a previous block would tweak the hash root and invalidate the whole Blockchain.

- Also, it would need all nodes in the Blockchain to delete the data simultaneously, which is not easy.

- GDPR requires user identity, whereas Blockchain deals with user anonymity.

As shown in Figure 2-1, one way to find a solution to this is to keep the personal and private data in an off-chain database and save only the hash value on the Blockchain. Any change in the off-chain database would lead to a change in hash value, which would mismatch with the hash value stored on the on-chain database (i.e., Blockchain). With this approach, the individual user can have full control of data, including addition, modification, and deletion.

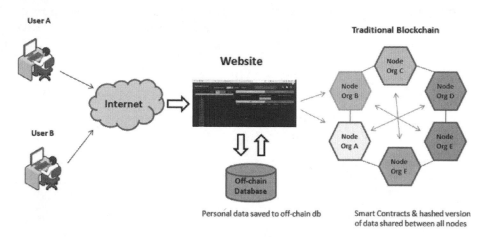

Figure 2-1. *Traditional Blockchain with GDPR compliance*

However, the issues with this approach are as follows:

- We cannot restore the historic or original data from Blockchain, as hashing is a one-way function.

- Data is broadcast to all nodes, even if they are nonparticipants in the transaction.

- Also, with this approach we are not leveraging the full functionality of Blockchain such as immutability, data security, replication, and much more.

- There is still no geographic restriction on data sharing, even if it's the hash value.

Corda's Compliance with GDPR

Corda is the perfect answer to a GDPR-compliant DLT. The Corda team has taken special care for data privacy compliance from Corda's inception, which many of its contemporary Enterprise Blockchain platforms had not.

As shown in Figure 2-2, in Corda personal data is shared across only the designated nodes. With self-sovereign KYC solutions built on Corda, individual users can log into a node and independently control their user data.

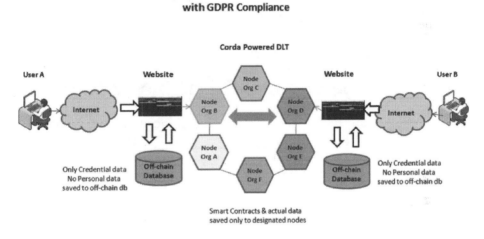

Figure 2-2. *Corda with GDPR compliance*

Corda's Differentiators, a Recap

Now that we have gone through the internal architecture of Corda, let's revisit and figure out what makes Corda the choice of most leading organizations for DLT space today.

No Global Sharing and No Central Database

In Corda, each node maintains a separate database of data that is only relevant to it. As a result, each peer sees only a subset of facts on the ledger, and no peer is aware of the ledger in its entirety.

No Global Broadcast

In Corda there is no concept of global broadcasting of data, and all communications are only on peer-to-peer basis. If you need to share the same information with multiple nodes, then you have to do it through coding, manually traversing a for loop. However, in a future release, this is planned to be introduced.

Blockchain Features and Yet No Blockchain

Corda does not come with blocks and it is not a Blockchain; yet it retains all the promises of a private permissioned Blockchain network, such as

- Immutability

- Traceability

- Replication

- Single source of truth for all involved parties

Real-Time Synchronous Transactions

As Corda is not a Blockchain, there is no waiting period for transactions to be added to a block and voting or any other consensus mechanism. Transactions are executed in a synchronous manner if validated and approved by all concerned nodes along with the notary, provided there is no double spending.

GDPR Complaint

Before Facebook's massive data breach affecting more than 87 million users, most of us were not aware that our personal data can be used by top-notch organizations for their business. Now that we are aware, many nations have come up with their own policies on consumers' private data; GDPR is one such practice followed in Europe. As per Wikipedia, "The General Data Protection Regulation 2016/679 is a regulation in EU law on data protection and privacy for all individuals within the European Union and the European Economic Area. It also addresses the export of personal data outside the EU and EEA areas." According to experts, it's the most important change in data privacy regulation in 20 years.

Obviously GDPR and the current generation of Blockchains are not compliant with each other. In traditional Blockchain, data is distributed to all nodes or some of the nodes even if those nodes are not the related parties participating in the transaction; this is true for public as well as many private permissioned and consortium Blockchains. However, Corda is a league apart; its architecture has taken care of this part long before GDPR was put into practice.

Quiz

1. Can a party keep the state data only with it?

    A. Yes

    B. No

2. Is a notary a single point of failure for Corda?

    A. Yes

    B. No

3. Which Blockchain features does Corda have?

    A. Immutability

    B. Traceability

    C. Replication

    D. All of the above

4. If I have to access today's exchange rate from a third party, which Corda utility/service I would use?

    A. Notary

    B. Oracle

    C. Contract

5. How many unconsumed states of any data be available on a vault?

    A. One

    B. Many

    C. None

Answers

1 A, 2 B, 3 D, 4 B, 5 A

References

1. Ricardian Contract (https://en.wikipedia.org/wiki/Ricardian_contract)

2. What Is a Ricardian Contract? (www.r3.com/blog/what-is-a-ricardian-contract/)

CHAPTER 3

Installation, Development, Deployment, Unit, and Functional Testing

This chapter is mostly targeted to developers who want to learn installation, programming, unit testing, deployment, and functional testing of the Corda ledger. This chapter also comes with a sample project that can be downloaded by developers.

Corda runs on Windows, Mac, and Debian/Ubuntu. For the installation of Corda, follow these steps:

1. Download and install Java 8 in your machine, and add the location of the bin folder of the JDK installation for the PATH variable in System Variables. You can check if Java is installed properly by checking "java -version" on the command line.

2. Download git from `https://git-scm.com/download` and install in your machine. Again, check up through "git --version" on your command line.

© Debajani Mohanty 2019
D. Mohanty, *R3 Corda for Architects and Developers*,
https://doi.org/10.1007/978-1-4842-4529-3_3

3. Download and install IntelliJ IDE from `www.jetbrains.com/idea/download/download-thanks.html?code=IIC`. This is the most suitable IDE to develop and run Corda.

Note   If you still need any help in setting up the machines, then the best place to start would be to watch the CordaBootcamp videos shown in Figure 3-1, which are freely available on YouTube (`www.youtube.com/playlist?list=PLi1PppB3-YrVq5Qy_RM9Qidq0eh-nL11N`).

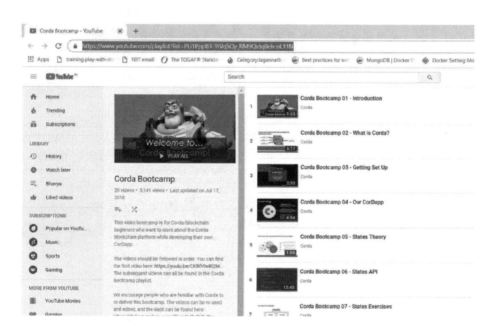

Figure 3-1. *Corda Bootcamp videos on YouTube*

The Corda community also arranges classroom as well as online sessions with CordaBootcamp, which is usually a one-day session. However, you should have some knowledge of Blockchain and expertise in Java to grasp it all in 6–8 hours. Now let's do it manually in the chapter. But first let's go through some of the core concepts.

States

The state class has to implement ContractState interface, which has only one method, namely, getParticipants(), which retrieves List<AbstractParty> (i.e., a list of abstract parties).

With each transaction, the data in the state object changes, and hence at any point of time a state object can have multiple historical versions and only one current version.

Any class that implements any of the subinterfaces of ContractState has to implement the getParticipants() method to return all the participants who wish to be notified for any change in the data in state object. ContractState can have the following different subinterfaces:

- LinearState

- OwnableState

- QueryableState

- SchedulableState

Note   A state must implement ContractState or one of its descendants.

LinearState

In Corda, which has Blockchain-like features, data is always immutable. However, same data can have multiple versions updated by each transaction that handles the data. For example, a property represented by a data object can have different owners updated with each new transaction. However, some unique data like the propertyId should remain the same for tracking the history of transactions. For such purposes, LinearState is used.

Any state class that implements the LinearState interface represents data that can change over time. This interface comes with a default primary key known as linearId, which is a UniqueIdentifier that remains unaltered, whereas other customized data in the object implementing LinearState can get updated in later states. At any point in time, the state can have many different versions, one of them being current and the rest being historical data. However, as already mentioned, all those versions would share the same linearId. This makes the audit trail and tracking process easier.

After this chapter, you can visit chapter 6 to learn how LinearState is used in a land registry use case.

OwnableState

The OwnableState interface stands for a state with an owner and is not associated with any unique ID as linearId. This interface has just one method, withNewOwner(), which has to be implemented by the state class.

One may wonder why someone even needs an OwnableState. Well, it's mostly used for fungible assets whose values or units may vary over a period of time and also can be interchanged, merged, and split. Let's say I have a fungible asset of some cryptocurrencies whose owner is me; in a future transaction I may pass it on to someone else as the new owner. You can visit https://github.com/kid101/EncumbranceDemo to find a fine example of OwnableState type of Cake and Expiry state objects.

QueryableState

Implementing QueryableState, the class can access the data in the database deployed in the individual node. It comes with two methods: supportedSchemas() and generateMappedObject(). The QueryableState interface uses schemas where all or part of the main state object are stored in a local database and can produce results to fine-tune vault queries from the API layer. You can visit the land registry project in the next chapter and find how QueryableState is used for fine-tuned queries on Corda.

SchedulableState

This is mostly used for event scheduling for future actions. The only method it has is nextScheduledActivity().

There are two more classes we must discuss that are part of almost all state objects.

CordaSerializable

It's interesting to note that not all data are permitted to be stored on Corda network. In order to whitelist only the data which are supposed to be saved, they have to be annotated with @CordaSerializable. However, all these states already do that, and hence implementing any of these states, our data in state class is marked as serializable.

Amount

The amount is a special type of class in Corda that is often a positive number associated with a currency: Amount<Currency> or asset.

Note that amounts of different tokens do not mix, and attempting to add or subtract two amounts of different currencies will throw IllegalArgumentException. Instead of representing actual value and currency fields separately, a clubbed value of amount fields is very frequently used in Corda for financial transactions.

Contract

The contract class has to implement a verify() method where we have to keep all our business logic.

Ricardian Contract

Corda uses Ricardian contracts, where prose like actual contract sentences is translated into code for validation of transactions in real time.

requireThat

As shown in Listing 3-1, using the requireThat() method, we can have any number of require.using() clauses, each of which takes a string to be used for the exception message, and an expression that will throw the exception if evaluated to true. Here, we grab the list of inputs from our transaction by calling getInputs() on our injected transaction variable tx, and then check to see if it's empty.

Listing 3-1. requireThat

```
if (tx.getInputStates().size() != 0)
    throw new IllegalArgumentException("Transactions must have
    zero inputs");
```

Commands

Commands contain signers, signing parties, and a value that differentiates types of command in the contract. Now the line in Listing 3-2 shows the commandType derived from the command inside the contract class.

Listing 3-2.

```
CommandData commandType = tx.getCommand(0).getValue();
```

Now, as shown in Listing 3-3, we can compare the value of this commandType, for example to check if it's a create or modify or cancel command and implements the relevant check in the verify() method.

Listing 3-3.

```
if (commandType instanceof Issue) {
    ..
    }
} else {
    throw new IllegalArgumentException("Transactions command
    must be of type Issue");
}
```

Time Windows

Sometimes the transactions have to be agreed by all parties within a particular time period. At that time, a "Time Window" is used with a start and end time that the notary keeps under observation. The transaction must be committed within that time period.

In the code in Listing 3-4, you can find a setTimeWindow() method with start and end times for committing the transaction. It can also have a constraint to start after a particular time with no end time or just an end time constraint.

Listing 3-4.

```
TransactionBuilder txBuilder = new TransactionBuilder(notary)
                .addOutputState(cake, SomeContract.SOME_
                CONTRACT_ID, notary, 1)
                .addCommand(new SomeContract.Commands.
                Create(), someAsset.getOwner().
                getOwningKey())
                .setTimeWindow(Instant.now(), Duration.
                ofSeconds(10));
```

We will see more examples with this method later in this chapter.

Attachment

Corda gives us the facility to transfer and store attachment files in the nodes. These attachments can be receipts, images, or shared data in PDF, jpg, doc, and similar formats; however, all such files have to be converted to zip or jar formats before saving. Refer to the eHospital project in chapter 7 for the implementation side of attachment.

LedgerTransaction

A LedgerTransaction is passed on to the contract with number of inputs, outputs, commands, attachments, notaries, and time windows. Inside contract's verify method, we do a validation check of all.

Flow

A flow represents the business flows that involve creating new states, validating them by contracts, and committing them all to the ledger. The call() is the default function of a flow between different nodes and is marked with the @Suspendable annotation. Flow framework in Corda has the option to run many active flows running in concurrency. These flows can go on even for days.

A flow involves a FlowLogic and TransactionBuilder class.

FlowLogic

FlowLogic<T> represents a business flow where we can update the ledger, do database activity, call another flow, and so on. Here <T> represents the class that it would return. A flow can be of many different types and can have subflows as well.

InitiatingFlow

If annotated as InitiatingFlow, it means the flow can be initiated on its own.

InitiatedBy

If annotated as InitiatedBy, it means that it is initiated by another flow and cannot be hit directly. Such a flow can have a FlowLogic<Unit> as the return type if we do not wish to return anything back to the caller of the flow.

StartableByRPC

If annotated as StartableByRPC, it means the flow can be initiated by RPC connection, which is the interface between the outside of a Corda node and its internals.

FinalityFlow

A transaction is finalized by a FinalityFlow, where the transaction is sent to notary and saved to all relevant vaults for local storage.

TransactionBuilder

Inside the call() method of a flow, a TransactionBuilder is used to create a transaction, which can involve input(s), output(s), command(s), time window(s), notaries, attachments, and so on.

ProgressTracker

In a business flow, ProgressTracker helps to trace the progress of an operation. Usually we define a number of progress tracker steps each with a label and get the report on the console.

Vault

Vault is the local database of the node where only the data relevant to that node or that owner gets saved. This data can be queried and retrieved as and when required. It's worth noting that this data can be of unconsumed (i.e., latest) or consumed (i.e., historic states) state objects. Hence, we can track all the transformations of state of a particular state object at any time. The queries can be done either on the basis of the liner ID or on any other parameter basis, which we will discuss in later in this chapter with example.

Oracles

We know that in a private permissioned distributed ledger such as Corda, all transactions happen within the network. However, what if we need data from some external services? For example, a particular transaction may need today's exchange rate for calculation of some payment. Oracles are network services that help us to bridge such gaps by connecting to the external world and getting us the information that we need in the transaction. They can also help in committing transactions in some external service if that is a requirement of the transaction.

Project Setup

Now please download the code from github with the following instruction on the command line. This in fact is the same project as taught in the CordaBootcamp video, but with a few modifications such as completing whatever code is missing in the original source (as instructed in the videos):

git clone "`https://github.com/`" URL provided by the Apress location"/bootcamp-cordapp.git"

Now open the IntelliJ IDEA IDE shown in Figure 3-2 and select "Import Project" to open the project.

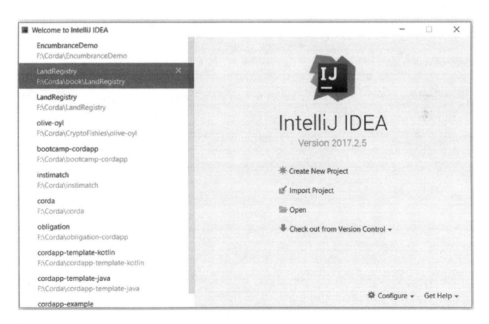

Figure 3-2. *Open IntelliJ IDEA IDE*

Then, choose the "Import project from external model" option, select "Gradle," and click "Next" as shown in Figure 3-3.

Figure 3-3. *Select Gradle on IntelliJ IDEA*

Finally, select the downloaded location of source code folder and click "Finish" as shown in Figure 3-4.

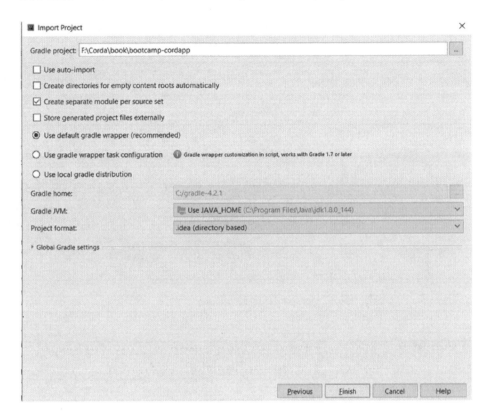

Figure 3-4. *Select location*

The project will show up on left-hand side as shown in Figure 3-5.

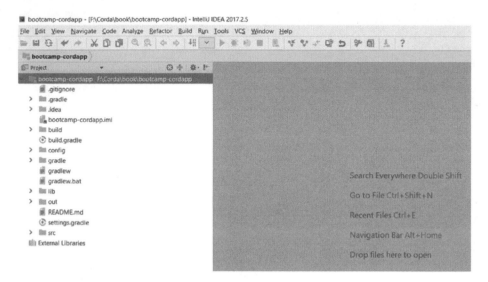

Figure 3-5. *Project on IntelliJ IDEA*

TDD in Corda: Unit Testing and More

Decentralized applications take much effort to get tested with all the nodes
up and running in real-life-like environments. It's crucial to unit test the
code and make sure that the contracts and flows are working as expected
in all positive, negative, and boundary conditions. Unit testing can be
done by using mock objects. In fact, Corda's unit testing model inspires
the adoption of a test-driven development (TDD) model where states,
contracts, and flows should be written and immediately unit tested before
running and testing in integration mode.

Corda API for Unit Testing

Corda provides full support for TDD for unit testing of contracts and states.
It also provides built-in mock services to unit test in complete isolation.
The following are a few.

MockServices

This interface helps us to write contract tests using the "ledger" method, with data and service isolation of each test with no side effects.

TestIdentity

This class represents a mocked node or party that encapsulates a test identity with a CordaX500Name (name of the individual or organization, as well as the country and locality) and a key pair, as well as a range of utility methods for use during testing.

Project Import Test

First run the ProjectImportedOKTest as shown in Figure 3-6 to check that the files have been retrieved properly and that the project is running fine.

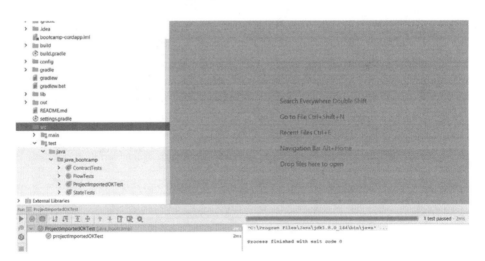

Figure 3-6. *ProjectImportedOKTest*

Unit Testing of State

Run StateTests as shown in Figure 3-7 to check that TokenState is working fine.

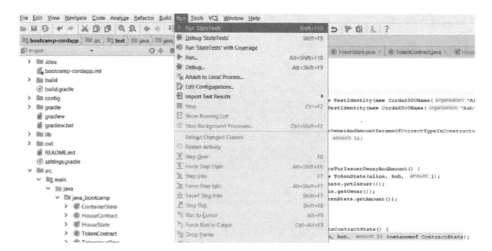

Figure 3-7. *Run StateTests*

You can see that StateTests.java has a few methods, all of which should pass as shown in Figure 3-8.

- tokenStateHasIssuerOwnerAndAmountParamsOf
  CorrectTypeInConstructor(): Checks if TokenState can
  be instantiated successfully

- tokenStateHasGettersForIssuerOwnerAndAmount():
  Checks if issuer, owner, and amount are set properly in
  the object

- tokenStateImplementsContractState(): Checks if the
  state object is actually an instance of ContractState
  interface

- tokenStateHasTwoParticipantsTheIssuerAndThe
  Owner(): Checks if the participants who would be
  notified when state is updated include Alice and Bob
  (i.e., the issuer and the borrower). Note this is because
  we have added both in the getParticipants() method in
  TokenState.java

Figure 3-8. *StateTests results*

Unit Testing of Contract

Then run ContractTests to unit test TokenContract.java. Initially, it will
throw "NotSerializableException." But then follow troubleshooting as
mentioned in the next section. In IntelliJ IDEA, go to File ➤ Settings
➤ Build, Execution, Deployment ➤ Compiler ➤ Java Compiler and
add -parameters to the Additional command-line parameters field.
A screenshot of the fix should be as shown in Figure 3-9.

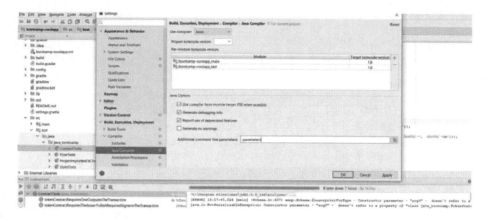

Figure 3-9. *Fix for running unit testing of contract*

Then completely rebuild the project (Build ➤ Rebuild Project). Now ContractTests will work.

Unit Testing of Flow

Now open the TokenIssueFlow.java in your IDE; you will find that the code is written in the call() method with the following flow as instructed in the Bootcamp video.

Now run the FlowTests to test the TokenIssueFlow.java. First you will get "java.lang.IllegalStateException: Missing the '-javaagent' JVM argument" error, as in Figure 3-10.

```
java.lang.IllegalStateException: Missing the '-javaagent' JVM argument. Make sure you run the tests with the Quasar java agent att
See https://docs.corda.net/troubleshooting.html - 'Fiber classes not instrumented' for more details.

    at net.corda.node.services.statemachine.StateMachineManagerImpl.checkQuasarJavaAgentPresence(StateMachineManagerImpl.kt:162)
    at net.corda.node.services.statemachine.StateMachineManagerImpl.start(StateMachineManagerImpl.kt:155)
    at net.corda.node.internal.AbstractNode$start$$inlined$apply$lambda$1.invoke(AbstractNode.kt:281)
    at net.corda.node.internal.AbstractNode$start$$inlined$apply$lambda$1.invoke(AbstractNode.kt:103)
    at net.corda.nodeapi.internal.persistence.CordaPersistence.inTopLevelTransaction(CordaPersistence.kt:148)
```

Figure 3-10. *IllegalStateException*

In order to resolve this, we have to do a small tweak in the setup on IntelliJ IDEA IDE. Click "Edit Configurations" on the FlowTests file as shown in Figure 3-11.

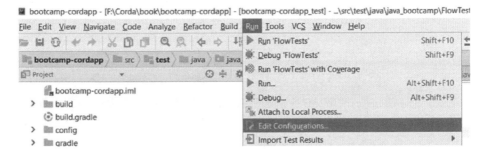

Figure 3-11. *Edit configurations*

Now on the configuration window, add the lines shown in Listing 3-5 and Figure 3-12 to the "VM options" edit box.

Listing 3-5.

```
-ea -javaagent:lib/quasar.jar
```

Note   The forward or backward slash depends upon the OS you are working in. I am doing so on Windows, hence using "/", whereas Mac and Linux users can use "\".

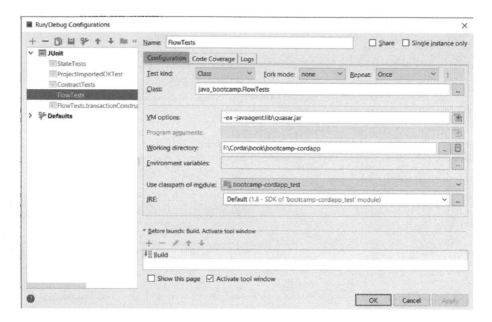

Figure 3-12. *VM options*

and click Apply and then the OK button. Now you can run the FlowTests and all tests should work.

Deploy and Run

Open a command-line interface and go to the folder where the project is stored. First run the command in Listing 3-6 to clean the previously created build folder.

Listing 3-6.

```
gradlew clean (FOR windows)
```

and then run the command shown in Listing 3-7 and Figure 3-13 to compile and deploy the nodes.

Listing 3-7.

```
gradlew deployNodes
or
gradlew deployNodesJava
```

Figure 3-13. *deployNodes*

Now you can see a build folder being created. Expand it and see the internals. You can find a folder against each node that you saw in build. gradle. For this project we have nodes named

- PartyA

- PartyB

- PartyC

- Notary

In order to add a new node to the Corda DLT network, the new node needs three keystores in its /build/nodes/[node name]/certificates/ folder:

- truststore.jks: acts as key store for the network root CA

- nodekeystore.jks: acts as key store of the node that secures identity key pairs

- certificatessslkeystore.jks: acts as the store for the node's TLS key pairs and certificates

Now on the same folder as in the preceding, run the command in Listing 3-8 to run the nodes.

Listing 3-8.

```
build\nodes\runnodes
```

You can see several windows getting spun as in Figure 3-14. They will take a few minutes to settle down before you can do more operations on them.

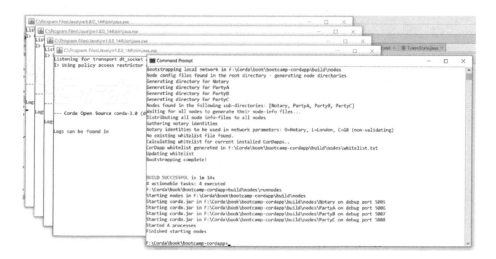

Figure 3-14. *runnodes*

Note that the build.gradle file in the project root has the most configurations related to Corda.

Now open the build.gradle file to check the configuration of nodes under "deployNodesJava" task. You can see that it has instructions to create a build folder in the "./build/nodes" location.

You can see that apart from the notary there are three more nodes named PartyA, PartyB, PartyC (i.e., four nodes in total).

One they are all up and running, type "flow list" on the command line and you can see all the flows in Listing 3-9 and Figure 3-15.

Listing 3-9.

```
Tue Nov 27 11:33:14 IST 2018>>> flow list
java_bootcamp.TokenIssueFlow
java_bootcamp.TwoPartyFlow
java_bootcamp.VerySimpleFlow
java_examples.IAmAFlowPair$IAmAFlow
net.corda.core.flows.ContractUpgradeFlow$Authorise
net.corda.core.flows.ContractUpgradeFlow$Deauthorise
net.corda.core.flows.ContractUpgradeFlow$Initiate
```

```
Tue Nov 27 11:33:14 IST 2018>>> flow list
java_bootcamp.TokenIssueFlow
java_bootcamp.TwoPartyFlow
java_bootcamp.VerySimpleFlow
java_examples.IAmAFlowPair$IAmAFlow
net.corda.core.flows.ContractUpgradeFlow$Authorise
net.corda.core.flows.ContractUpgradeFlow$Deauthorise
net.corda.core.flows.ContractUpgradeFlow$Initiate

Tue Nov 27 11:33:53 IST 2018>>> _
```

Figure 3-15. *Flow list*

You can start your flow from here. Please watch the format, which must be strictly followed as per the number of input parameters. Type the following flow instructions on the command line of Party A. Now to begin with, let's enter the parameters as shown in Listing 3-10.

Listing 3-10.

```
flow start TokenIssueFlow
```

Of course, it throws an error with a "No matching constructor found" message, as shown in Figure 3-16.

```
Wed Nov 28 19:28:43 IST 2018>>> flow start TokenIssueFlow
No matching constructor found:
- [owner: Party, amount: int]: missing parameter owner

Wed Nov 28 19:33:29 IST 2018>>>
```

Figure 3-16. *TokenIssueFlow with exception*

Now type the corrected flow instructions shown in Listing 3-11 and Figure 3-17 on the command line of Party A.

Listing 3-11.

```
flow start TokenIssueFlow owner: PartyB, amount: 99
```

```
Wed Nov 28 19:31:55 IST 2018>>> flow start TokenIssueFlow owner: PartyB, amount: 99
Done

Wed Nov 28 19:32:54 IST 2018>>>
```

Figure 3-17. *TokenIssueFlow running successfully*

Open the TokenIssueFlow.java file in the IDE and check its details. Note that the order of parameters in the command line should be exactly same as the order in the constructor in TokenIssueFlow.

Vault Query

A vault query is Corda's inherent mechanism to check the data immediately from the interactive shell. Now let's see the newly created state details through a vaultQuery. Type the command shown in Listing 3-12 on the interactive shell for Node A or Node B.

Listing 3-12.

```
Fri Nov 30 09:47:41 IST 2018>>> run vaultQuery
contractStateType: java_bootcamp.TokenState
```

and see the output as shown in Listing 3-13 and Figure 3-18.

Listing 3-13.

```
{
  "states" : [ {
    "state" : {
      "data" : {
        "owner" : "O=PartyB, L=New York, C=US",
        "issuer" : "O=PartyA, L=London, C=GB",
        "amount" : 99,
        "participants" : [ "O=PartyA, L=London, C=GB",
                           "O=PartyB, L=New York, C=US" ]
      },
      "contract" : "java_bootcamp.TokenContract",
      "notary" : "O=Notary, L=London, C=GB",
      "encumbrance" : null,
      "constraint" : {
        "attachmentId" : "7EC3EBB030D69508F9B70C8F49A16A2524
                          D088FDA7F5DB9AA595B882530FF8E8"
      }
    },
```

```
    "ref" : {
      "txhash" : "597A28E016D8A6A91D72A57A944C417DF529DD0A4DFC8
              D7A47FAC78BEDD656ED",
      "index" : 0
    }
  } ],
  "statesMetadata" : [ {
    "ref" : {
      "txhash" : "597A28E016D8A6A91D72A57A944C417DF529DD0A4DFC8
              D7A47FAC78BEDD656ED",
      "index" : 0
    },
    "contractStateClassName" : "java_bootcamp.TokenState",
    "recordedTime" : 1543551461.190000000,
    "consumedTime" : null,
    "status" : "UNCONSUMED",
    "notary" : "O=Notary, L=London, C=GB",
    "lockId" : null,
    "lockUpdateTime" : null
  } ],
  "totalStatesAvailable" : -1,
  "stateTypes" : "UNCONSUMED",
  "otherResults" : [ ]
}
```

```
Fri Nov 30 09:46:38 IST 2018>>> Jolokia: Agent started with URL http://127.0.0.1:7006/jolokia/
flow start TokenIssueFlow owner: PartyB, amount: 99
Done

Fri Nov 30 09:47:41 IST 2018>>> run vaultQuery contractStateType: java_bootcamp.TokenState
{
  "states" : [ {
    "state" : {
      "data" : {
        "owner" : "O=PartyB, L=New York, C=US",
        "issuer" : "O=PartyA, L=London, C=GB",
        "amount" : 99,
        "participants" : [ "O=PartyA, L=London, C=GB", "O=PartyB, L=New York, C=US" ]
      },
      "contract" : "java_bootcamp.TokenContract",
      "notary" : "O=Notary, L=London, C=GB",
      "encumbrance" : null,
      "constraint" : {
        "attachmentId" : "7EC3EBB030D69508F9B70C8F49A16A2524D088FDA7F5DB9AA595B882530FF8E8"
      }
    },
    "ref" : {
      "txhash" : "597A28E016D8A6A91D72A57A944C417DF529DD0A4DFC8D7A47FAC78BEDD656ED",
      "index" : 0
    }
  } ],
  "statesMetadata" : [ {
    "ref" : {
      "txhash" : "597A28E016D8A6A91D72A57A944C417DF529DD0A4DFC8D7A47FAC78BEDD656ED",
      "index" : 0
    },
    "contractStateClassName" : "java_bootcamp.TokenState",
    "recordedTime" : 1543551461.190000000,
    "consumedTime" : null,
    "status" : "UNCONSUMED",
    "notary" : "O=Notary, L=London, C=GB",
    "lockId" : null,
    "lockUpdateTime" : null
  } ],
  "totalStatesAvailable" : -1,
  "stateTypes" : "UNCONSUMED",
  "otherResults" : [ ]
}

Fri Nov 30 09:48:56 IST 2018>>>
```

Figure 3-18. *vaultQuery*

You can see details as owner, issuer, amount, contract class, state class, notary, txhash (or transaction ID), status, and so on in this state detail.

However if you try the same vault query on Node C, then you can see an empty state as shown in Listing 3-14 and Figure 3-19.

Listing 3-14.

```
Fri Nov 30 09:46:33 IST 2018>>> Jolokia: Agent started with URL
http://127.0.0.1:7008/jolokia/
run vaultQuery contractStateType: java_bootcamp.TokenState
{
  "states" : [ ],
  "statesMetadata" : [ ],
  "totalStatesAvailable" : -1,
  "stateTypes" : "UNCONSUMED",
  "otherResults" : [ ]
}
```

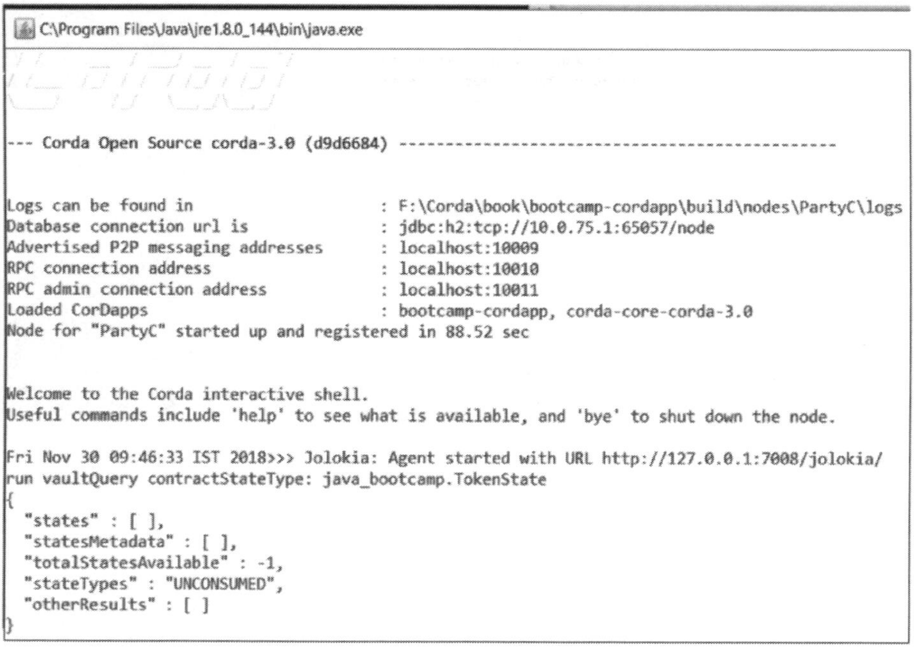

Figure 3-19. *vaultQuery shows no data for nonparticipating nodes*

We can add a web interface in front of this flow layer and expose it as a REpresentational State Transfer (REST) endpoint that the front end can hit for different kinds of services.

Exposing REST Endpoints for Integration with UI

You can use REST API to expose different services. You can use any front-end technology like angular, reactjs, or simple Java Server Pages (JSP) to integrate with the API layer. Now download the LandRegistry project, which is elaborated in the next chapter with the "gitclone .." command from the Apress location.

If you open that project in IntelliJ IDEA as shown in Figure 3-20, you will find two different folders:

- cordapp: contains API class where we expose REST endpoints and flows. You can optionally have a plug-in class for attaching endpoints with front-end code. You can create a separate front-end project also. In the LandRegistry project in the next chapter, you can find how API class is used to expose REST endpoints

- cordapp-contracts-states: contains all states and contracts

Figure 3-20. *Project layouts*

You have to run the same commands as before: "gradlew clean" and "gradlewdeployNodes" followed by "build\nodes\runnodes" to get the servers up and running before you start testing.

Functional Testing

Functional testing can be done in two different ways before integrating the endpoints with UI.

- Through REST calls

- Through nodes

Let's try both ways to test the functionality of the DApp.

Test Through REST Calls

The nodes take a little while (perhaps minutes) to run, and once they are up you can interact with them. First, let's see if the data is actually stored in the Corda ledger. In the absence of a proper UI, you can test it using a REST client. There are many REST clients available on the market; I have used "Advanced REST Client" or ARC for Chrome browser.

Now hit the REST API with getAllCurrentPropertyDetails endpoint as shown in Figure 3-21.

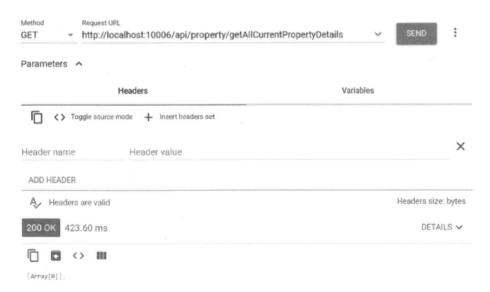

Figure 3-21. *TokenIssueFlow with exception*

It won't return any data as we have not added any.

Test Through Nodes

Now run the vault query on any of the nodes to check data; the command is as shown in Listing 3-15.

Listing 3-15.

```
run vaultQuery contractStateType: com.landRegistry.states.
PropertyDetails
```

The output will be blank in the beginning, as shown in Listing 3-16 and Figure 3-22.

Listing 3-16.

```
{
  "states" : [ ],
  "statesMetadata" : [ ],
  "totalStatesAvailable" : -1,
  "stateTypes" : "UNCONSUMED",
  "otherResults" : [ ]
}
```

```
--- Corda Open Source 3.1-corda (d193dd8) -----------------------------------------

Logs can be found in                       : F:\Corda\LandRegistry\build\nodes\InsuranceCompany\logs
Database connection url is                 : jdbc:h2:tcp://10.0.75.1:53923/node
Advertised P2P messaging addresses         : localhost:10015
RPC connection address                     : localhost:10016
RPC admin connection address               : localhost:10017
Loaded CorDapps                            : cordapp-0.1, cordapp-contracts-states-0.1, LandRegistry-0.1, corda-core-3.1-co
rda
Node for "InsuranceCompany" started up and registered in 154.3 sec


Welcome to the Corda interactive shell.
Useful commands include 'help' to see what is available, and 'bye' to shut down the node.

Tue Oct 16 06:47:39 IST 2018>>> Jolokia: Agent started with URL http://127.0.0.1:7007/jolokia/

Tue Oct 16 07:26:06 IST 2018>>> run vaultQuery contractStateType: com.landRegistry.states.PropertyDetails
{
  "states" : [ ],
  "statesMetadata" : [ ],
  "totalStatesAvailable" : -1,
  "stateTypes" : "UNCONSUMED",
  "otherResults" : [ ]
}

Tue Oct 16 07:26:40 IST 2018>>>
```

Figure 3-22. *No output data on vaultQuery*

Now we have to insert data to the DLT and check the same functionality. First, run the command shown in Listing 3-17 onLandDepartment node

Listing 3-17.

```
flow list
```

and it will return the flows shown in Listing 3-18 and Figure 3-23.

Listing 3-18.

```
com.landRegistry.flows.ApprovePropertyFlow
com.landRegistry.flows.InitiatePropertyFlow
com.landRegistry.flows.TransferPropertyFlow
net.corda.core.flows.ContractUpgradeFlow$Authorise
net.corda.core.flows.ContractUpgradeFlow$Deauthorise
net.corda.core.flows.ContractUpgradeFlow$Initiate
```

Figure 3-23. *Flow list*

Now we need to start the actual flow with the next command. Please keep the format of parameters the same as in the sample instruction in Listing 3-19.

Listing 3-19.

```
flow start InitiatePropertyFlow propertyId: 1, propertyAddress:
some address, propertyPrice: 12000, buyerId: 1, sellerId: 2,
updatedBy: me, updatedTime: some time, owner: LandDepartment
```

and it will respond with "Done" if it's successful, as shown in Figure 3-24.

```
Tue Oct 16 05:56:03 IST 2018>>> flow start InitiatePropertyFlow propertyId: 1, propertyAddress: some address, propertyPr
ice: 12000, buyerId: 1, sellerId: 2, updatedBy: me, updatedTime: some time, owner: LandDepartment
Done
```

Figure 3-24. *Successful InitiatePropertyFlow run*

Now again, hit the REST API with getAllCurrentPropertyDetails endpoint and see the output. This will be discussed in more detail in the next chapter.

Troubleshooting

I found many known issues while coding, for which you can refer to the following web page. Refresh the project and build every time you change anything in the setting to take effect.

```
https://github.com/corda/bootcamp-cordapp/wiki/Troubleshooting
```

Use Cases

Now that you have learned the basics of Corda development, let's do some real assignments that will guide you to implement the same in real projects. I have added a few use cases as per market demand. If you refer to the diagram by Gartner at `https://strategiccoin.com/crypto-media-bites-on-gartner-data-doesnt-provide-perspective/`, the Blockchain consulting engagements could be divided into the following verticals.

- Finance

- Insurance

- Travel

- Manufacturing and supply chain

- Healthcare

- Telecommunication services

- Tokenization

- Agriculture

- Government/land registry

We will cover one or two use cases in each of these verticals in later chapters.

Quiz

1. What are the different installable software packages in Corda?

   A. Community

   B. Enterprise

   C. Both

2. A linearId is mandatory in which contract state subinterface in Corda?

   A. LinearState

   B. OwnableState

3. What are the different methods in the contract interface in Corda?

   A. Validate

   B. Verify

   C. Check

   D. Contract interface in Corda does not have any methods; it's a marker interface

4. Does Corda support attachments?

   A. Yes

   B. No

5. Can we broadcast state data to multiple nodes in Corda?

   A. Yes

   B. No

6. To represent fungible assets, what kind of state object do we use?

   A. LinearState

   B. OwnableState

   C. QueryableState

   D. SchedulableState

7. A call() method in a flow must be annotated with which of the following?

   A. @Suspendable

   B. @CordaSerializable

Answers

1 C, 2 A, 3 B, 4 A, 5 A, 6 B, 7 A

Reference

Test Driven Development for Blockchain Apps with R3 Corda — How to Write Contracts and Unit Tests (https://medium.com/corda/test-driven-development-for-blockchain-apps-with-r3-corda-how-to-write-contracts-and-unit-tests-f2360fe7a97d)

CHAPTER 4

Government and Real Estate

In this chapter, we will learn how Corda can be used as a private permissioned ledger for recording the transactions between different parties in land registry expediting business processes and bringing transparency to the entire ecosystem. This chapter also comes with a sample project that can be downloaded by developers.

Fraud is very high in land- and property-related transactions. This is often due to the fact that even if someone claims to be the rightful owner of a piece of land, he/she might have been duped by another seller who sold the property with fake documents. Also, tracking of the property deal and the ownership history of the property are crucial in property transactions.

Let's consider a scenario where a property is to be transferred between two different persons. It might involve multiple independent organizations such as a land registry department, a bank, a surveyor, and so on. In the past, such workflows were a paper-based system that consumed a huge amount of time for completion. Nowadays, many organizations have digitized the entire system and yet the basic issue has remained the same. Organizations participating in the workflow do not wish to share their data for a common platform, and hence tracking the transactions at any point of time has always been a challenge.

© Debajani Mohanty 2019
D. Mohanty, *R3 Corda for Architects and Developers*,
https://doi.org/10.1007/978-1-4842-4529-3_4

Solution

Land registry is the right kind of use case valid for Blockchain implementation, and most Blockchain protocols have tried their hands at this use case. The beauty of Blockchain is that once stored, data can't be modified or deleted, which gives Blockchain and distributed ledger technology (DLT) the edge over any other traditional database. Let's find out how to trace out all the previously recorded ownership from Corda DLT.

As shown in Figure 4-1, let's create a decentralized application based on Corda DLT where traceability can be closely monitored by the underlying sharable ledger.

Let's say the different parties in this kind of deal are as follows:

- Land department

- Third-party surveyor

- Bank

- Insurance company

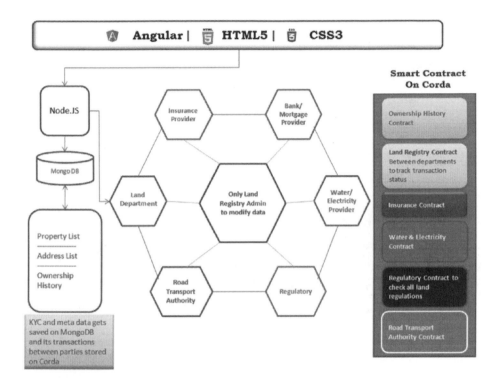

Figure 4-1. *Land registry system architecture*

The transaction flows will be as follows:

1. The buyer and seller approach the land department, which creates a new land registry case with existing property ID. If the property is a first-time property, then the property ID has to be generated before processing the deal.

2. The land department assigns the property details to a third-party surveyor to survey the details of the property.

3. The surveyor approves and sends back to land department or rejects with reasons.

4. Upon positive response from the surveyor, the land department sends details to the bank for successful initiation of mortgage.

5. The bank approves and sends back to the land department or rejects with reasons.

6. Upon positive response from the bank, the land department transfers the ownership from seller to buyer.

We can add more parties in real life such as insurance company, water/gas/electricity departments for utility connections, and so on. Please note that we can join this with a B2C web application where the buyer and seller will be registered through some off-chain database like Oracle, mysql, or mongo, where there has to be a stringent KYC process for background verification and user IDs are created against each of them. The area elaborated in the preceding covers only the B2B transactions and uses those IDs of buyer and seller provided through the off-chain database.

In Corda, the order of execution is as follows:

API class -> Flow class -> State class & Contract class -> Data committed to ledger.

However, the queries do not need to follow this path. We can directly write queries in the API layer itself. So in our example we have an execution order for new property as follows:

PropertyTransferApi.initiatePropertyTransaction()-> InitiatePropertyFlow

-> PropertyDetails -> PropertyDetailsSchemaV1

-> PropertyContract

Let's elaborate this further.

Note   You can download the code from the repository associated with the book.

First we have to create a state class PropertyDetails with all the required data (propertyId, propertyAddress, propertyPrice, buyerId, sellerId, isMortgageApproved, isSurveyorApproved, owner, description, updatedBy, updatedTime, etc.).

In Listing 4-1, you can find the code for PropertyDetails.java. Note this class is of type *LinearState*. In LinearState, as we discussed before, there is a linearId of type UniqueIdentifier whose value remains the same, just like a primary key in a table which helps to track the object and its change of states. This state also implements *QueryableState*, which helps us to do many fine-tuned queries on the local data stored in the node in the form of a table.

Listing 4-1. PropertyDetails implementing LinearState and QueryableState Interfaces

```
package com.landRegistry.states;

import com.google.common.collect.ImmutableList;
import com.landRegistry.schema.PropertyDetailsSchemaV1;
import net.corda.core.contracts.LinearState;
import net.corda.core.contracts.UniqueIdentifier;
import net.corda.core.identity.AbstractParty;
import net.corda.core.identity.Party;
import net.corda.core.schemas.MappedSchema;
import net.corda.core.schemas.PersistentState;
import net.corda.core.schemas.QueryableState;
import net.corda.core.serialization.
ConstructorForDeserialization;
import org.jetbrains.annotations.NotNull;

import java.util.List;
import java.util.Objects;

public class PropertyDetails implements LinearState,
QueryableState {
```

```java
    private final int propertyId;
    private final String propertyAddress;
    private final int propertyPrice;
    private final int buyerId;
    private final int sellerId;
    private final boolean isMortgageApproved;
    private final boolean isSurveyorApproved;
    private final Party owner;
    private final String description;
    private final String updatedBy;
    private final String updatedTime;

    private final UniqueIdentifier linearId;

    public PropertyDetails(int propertyId,
                           String propertyAddress, int property
                           Price, int buyerId, int sellerId,
                           boolean isMortgageApproved, boolean
                           boolean isSurveyorApproved, boolean
                           isSurveyorApproved, Party owner,
                           String description, String updatedBy,
                           String updatedTime) {
        this.propertyId = propertyId;
        this.owner = owner;
        this.propertyAddress = propertyAddress;
        this.propertyPrice = propertyPrice;
        this.buyerId = buyerId;
        this.sellerId = sellerId;
        this.isMortgageApproved = isMortgageApproved;
        this.isSurveyorApproved = isSurveyorApproved;
        this.description = description;
        this.updatedBy = updatedBy;

        this.updatedTime = updatedTime;
```

```
    this.linearId = new UniqueIdentifier();
}

@ConstructorForDeserialization
public PropertyDetails(int propertyId, String property
                       Address, int propertyPrice, int
                       buyerId, int sellerId, boolean
                       isMortgageApproved, boolean
                       isSurveyorApproved, Party owner,
                       String description, String updatedBy,
                       String updatedTime, UniqueIdentifier
                       linearId) {
    this.propertyId = propertyId;
    this.owner = owner;
    this.propertyAddress = propertyAddress;
    this.propertyPrice = propertyPrice;
    this.buyerId = buyerId;
    this.sellerId = sellerId;
    this.isMortgageApproved = isMortgageApproved;
    this.isSurveyorApproved = isSurveyorApproved;
    this.description = description;
    this.updatedBy = updatedBy;
    this.updatedTime = updatedTime;

    this.linearId = linearId;
}

@NotNull
public List<AbstractParty> getParticipants() {
    return ImmutableList.of(owner);
}

public PropertyDetails transfer(Party newOwner) {
```

```
        return new PropertyDetails(propertyId, propertyAddress,
                propertyPrice, buyerId, sellerId, isMortgage
                Approved, isSurveyorApproved, newOwner,
                description, updatedBy, updatedTime, linearId);
    }

    public PropertyDetails approvedByBank(boolean isApproved) {
        return new PropertyDetails(propertyId, propertyAddress,
                propertyPrice, buyerId, sellerId, isApproved,
                isSurveyorApproved, owner, description, updatedBy,
                updatedTime, linearId);
    }

    public PropertyDetails approvedBySurveyor(boolean isApproved) {
        return new PropertyDetails(propertyId, propertyAddress,
                propertyPrice, buyerId, sellerId, isMortgage
                Approved, isApproved, owner, description,
                updatedBy, updatedTime, linearId);
    }

    public Party getOwner() {
        return owner;
    }

    public int getPropertyId() {
        return propertyId;
    }

    public String getPropertyAddress() {
        return propertyAddress;
    }

    public int getPropertyPrice() {
```

```java
        return propertyPrice;
    }

    public int getBuyerId() {
        return buyerId;
    }

    public int getSellerId() {
        return sellerId;
    }

    public boolean isMortgageApproved() {
        return isMortgageApproved;
    }

    public boolean isSurveyorApproved() {
        return isSurveyorApproved;
    }

    public String getDescription() {
        return description;
    }

    public String getUpdatedBy() {
        return updatedBy;
    }

    public String getUpdatedTime() {
        return updatedTime;
    }

    @NotNull
    public UniqueIdentifier getLinearId() {
        return linearId;
    }
```

```java
@Override
public boolean equals(Object o) {
    if (this == o) return true;
    if (o == null || getClass() != o.getClass()) return false;
    PropertyDetails that = (PropertyDetails) o;
    return propertyId == that.propertyId &&
            propertyAddress == that.propertyAddress &&
            propertyPrice == that.propertyPrice &&
            owner.equals(that.owner) &&
            buyerId == that.buyerId &&
            sellerId == that.sellerId &&
            isMortgageApproved == that.isMortgageApproved &&
            isSurveyorApproved == that.isSurveyorApproved &&
            description.equals(that.description) &&
            updatedBy.equals(that.updatedBy) &&
            updatedTime.equals(that.updatedTime) &&
            linearId.equals(that.linearId);
}

@Override
public int hashCode() {
    return Objects.hash(propertyId, propertyAddress, buyerId,
            sellerId, isMortgageApproved, isSurveyorApproved,
            owner, description, updatedBy, updatedTime,
            linearId);
}

@NotNull
@Override
public Iterable<MappedSchema> supportedSchemas() {
    return ImmutableList.of(new PropertyDetailsSchemaV1());
}
```

```java
@NotNull
@Override
public PersistentState generateMappedObject(MappedSchema
schema) {
    if (schema instanceof PropertyDetailsSchemaV1) {
        return new PropertyDetailsSchemaV1.
        PersistentPropertyDetails(
                this.propertyId,
                this.propertyAddress,
                this.propertyPrice,
                this.buyerId,
                this.linearId.getId());
    } else {
        throw new IllegalArgumentException("Unrecognised
        schema $schema");
    }
}
}
```

You can find two methods named supportedSchemas() and generateMappedObject(), which are default methods and must be implemented for QueryableState.

Now in Listing 4-2, let's check the details of PropertyDetailsSchemaV1.java.

Listing 4-2. PropertyDetailsSchema for persisting selected and mapped data on ledger

```java
package com.landRegistry.schema;

import com.google.common.collect.ImmutableList;
import net.corda.core.schemas.MappedSchema;
import net.corda.core.schemas.PersistentState;
```

```java
import javax.persistence.Column;
import javax.persistence.Entity;
import javax.persistence.Table;
import java.util.UUID;

/**
 * An PropertyDetails Schema.
 */
public class PropertyDetailsSchemaV1 extends MappedSchema {
    public PropertyDetailsSchemaV1() {
        super(PropertyDetailsSchemaV1.class, 1, ImmutableList.
        of(PersistentPropertyDetails.class));
    }

    @Entity
    @Table(name = "land_registry_states")
    public static class PersistentPropertyDetails extends
    PersistentState {
        @Column(name = "propertyId")
        private final int propertyId;
        @Column(name = "propertyAddress")
        private final String propertyAddress;
        @Column(name = "propertyPrice")
        private final int propertyPrice;
        @Column(name = "buyerId")
        private final int buyerId;
        @Column(name = "linear_id")
        private final UUID linearId;
```

```java
    public PersistentPropertyDetails(int propertyId,
                                     String propertyAddress,
                                     int propertyPrice,
                                     int buyerId,
                                     UUID linearId) {
        this.propertyId = propertyId;
        this.propertyAddress = propertyAddress;
        this.propertyPrice = propertyPrice;
        this.buyerId = buyerId;
        this.linearId = linearId;
    }

    // Default constructor required by hibernate.
    public PersistentPropertyDetails() {
        this.propertyId = 0;
        this.propertyAddress = null;
        this.propertyPrice = 0;
        this.buyerId = 0;
        this.linearId = null;
    }
  }
}
```

In PropertyDetailsSchemaV1.java, we have the flexibility of storing either all or part of the variables as original PropertyDetails object. This data is saved to a local land_registry_states table. Do not forget to implement a blank constructor, which is a basic requirement without which it would not work.

In Listing 4-3, find the contract class, which has minimal validations, but you can add all kinds of checks for business validations here.

Listing 4-3. PropertyContract verifying input/output data in a transaction

```java
package com.landRegistry.contracts;

import com.google.common.collect.ImmutableList;
import com.landRegistry.states.PropertyDetails;
import net.corda.core.contracts.CommandWithParties;
import net.corda.core.contracts.Contract;
import net.corda.core.identity.Party;
import net.corda.core.transactions.LedgerTransaction;

import static net.corda.core.contracts.ContractsDSL.
requireSingleCommand;
import static net.corda.core.contracts.ContractsDSL.
requireThat;

public class PropertyContract implements Contract {
    public static final String ID = "com.landRegistry.
    contracts.PropertyContract";

    public void verify(LedgerTransaction tx) throws
    IllegalArgumentException {
        verifyAll(tx);
    }

    private void verifyAll(LedgerTransaction tx) throws
    IllegalArgumentException {
        CommandWithParties<PropertyCommands> command
        = requireSingleCommand(tx.getCommands(),
        PropertyCommands.class);
        PropertyCommands commandType = command.getValue();
        if (commandType instanceof PropertyCommands.Create)
        verifyCreate(tx, command);
```

```java
    else if (commandType instanceof PropertyCommands.
    Transfer) verifyTransfer(tx, command);
    else if (commandType instanceof PropertyCommands.
    BankApproval) verifyBankApproval(tx, command);
}

private void verifyCreate(LedgerTransaction tx,
CommandWithParties command) throws IllegalArgumentException {
    requireThat(require -> {
        require.using("A Property Transfer transaction
        should consume no input states.",
                tx.getInputs().isEmpty());
        require.using("A Property Transfer transaction
        should only create one output state.",
                tx.getOutputs().size() == 1);

        final PropertyDetails out = tx.outputsOfType(Proper
        tyDetails.class).get(0);
        return null;
    });
}

private void verifyTransfer(LedgerTransaction tx,
CommandWithParties command) throws IllegalArgumentException {
    requireThat(require -> {
        require.using("A Property Transfer transaction
        should only consume one input state.",
                tx.getInputs().size() == 1);
        require.using("A Property Transfer transaction
        should only create one output state.",
                tx.getOutputs().size() == 1);
        final PropertyDetails in = tx.inputsOfType
        (PropertyDetails.class).get(0);
```

113

```
        final PropertyDetails out = tx.outputsOfType(Proper
        tyDetails.class).get(0);

        require.using("The owner Property must change in a
        Property Transfer transaction.",
                in.getOwner() != out.getOwner());

        require.using("There must only be one signer (the
        current owner) in a Property Transfer transaction.",
                command.getSigners().size() == 1);

        return null;
    });
}

private void verifyBankApproval(LedgerTransaction tx,
CommandWithParties command) throws IllegalArgumentException {
    requireThat(require -> {
        //Add some more checks on your own
        return null;
    });
}
}
```

In Listing 4-4, find InitiatePropertyFlow.java, where we can see how the new PropertyDetails object is created and added as an output state to the TransactionBuilder. We have added a setTimeWindow() to mandate the signature of the notary service within the specified time limit of 10 seconds. At the end, we find a VerifySignAndFinaliseFlow, which again calls the FinalityFlow that verifies the transaction and sends it to the notary, which checks the transaction and agrees or disagrees. Upon acceptance by the notary, the transaction is finally committed to the ledger.

Listing 4-4. InitiatePropertyFlow to start a new property workflow

```java
package com.landRegistry.flows;

import co.paralleluniverse.fibers.Suspendable;
import com.landRegistry.contracts.PropertyCommands;
import com.landRegistry.contracts.PropertyContract;
import com.landRegistry.states.PropertyDetails;
import net.corda.core.flows.*;
import net.corda.core.identity.Party;
import net.corda.core.transactions.SignedTransaction;
import net.corda.core.transactions.TransactionBuilder;
import net.corda.core.utilities.ProgressTracker;
import net.corda.core.utilities.ProgressTracker.Step;

import java.time.Duration;
import java.time.Instant;

@InitiatingFlow
@StartableByRPC
public class InitiatePropertyFlow extends
FlowLogic<SignedTransaction> {
    private final Party owner;
    private final int propertyId;
    private final String propertyAddress;
    private final int propertyPrice;
    private final int buyerId;
    private final int sellerId;
    private final String updatedBy;
    private final String updatedTime;

    private final Step GENERATING_TRANSACTION = new
    Step("Generating transaction based on new PropertyDetails.");
```

```
private final Step SIGNING_TRANSACTION = new Step("Signing
transaction with our private key.");

private final Step FINALISING_TRANSACTION = new Step
("Obtaining notary signature and recording transaction.") {
    @Override
    public ProgressTracker childProgressTracker() {
        return FinalityFlow.Companion.tracker();
    }
};

// The progress tracker checkpoints each stage of the flow
    and outputs the specified messages when each
// checkpoint is reached in the code.

private final ProgressTracker progressTracker = new
ProgressTracker(
        GENERATING_TRANSACTION,
        SIGNING_TRANSACTION,
        FINALISING_TRANSACTION
);

public InitiatePropertyFlow(int propertyId, String property
                            Address, int propertyPrice, int
                            buyerId, int sellerId, String
                            updatedBy, String updatedTime,
                            Party owner) {
    this.propertyId = propertyId;
    this.propertyAddress = propertyAddress;
    this.propertyPrice = propertyPrice;
    this.owner = owner;
    this.buyerId = buyerId;
```

```
    this.sellerId = sellerId;
    this.updatedBy = updatedBy;
    this.updatedTime = updatedTime;
}
@Override
public ProgressTracker getProgressTracker() {
    return progressTracker;
}

@Suspendable
public SignedTransaction call() throws FlowException {
    Party notary = getServiceHub().getNetworkMapCache().
    getNotaryIdentities().get(0);

    progressTracker.setCurrentStep(GENERATING_TRANSACTION);
    PropertyDetails propertyDetails = new
    PropertyDetails(propertyId,
            propertyAddress,
            propertyPrice,
            buyerId,
            sellerId,
            false,
            false,
            owner,
            "New Property Transaction Initiated",
            updatedBy,
            updatedTime);

    progressTracker.setCurrentStep(SIGNING_TRANSACTION);
    TransactionBuilder builder = new
    TransactionBuilder(notary)
            .addOutputState(propertyDetails,
            PropertyContract.ID)
```

```
                        .addCommand(new PropertyCommands.Create(),
                        getOurIdentity().getOwningKey())
                        .setTimeWindow(Instant.now(), Duration.
                        ofSeconds(10));
              //We are adding a time window of 10 seconds for the Notary
                 service to sign the transaction replacing default one
              //This setWindow() is completely optional

              progressTracker.setCurrentStep(FINALISING_TRANSACTION);
              return subFlow(new VerifySignAndFinaliseFlow(builder));
        }
}
```

Finally, in Listing 4-5 we have the PropertyTransferApi.java. In this file, we can see that the first method, getAllCurrentPropertyDetails(), retrieves all the current states of PropertyDetails objects.

The second method, getAllPropertyDetailsForId(), retrieves all of the consumed/historic states as well as the unconsumed/current states of the PropertyDetails object.

The third method, getBidOffersOfPriceRange()/actually uses QueryableState to get fine-tuned search results.

Listing 4-5. PropertyTransferApi exposing API endpoints through REST based web services

```
package com.landRegistry.api;

import com.landRegistry.bean.PropertyDetailsBean;
import com.landRegistry.flows.ApprovePropertyFlow;
import com.landRegistry.flows.InitiatePropertyFlow;
import com.landRegistry.flows.TransferPropertyFlow;
import com.landRegistry.schema.PropertyDetailsSchemaV1;
import com.landRegistry.states.PropertyDetails;
import net.corda.core.contracts.StateAndRef;
```

```java
import net.corda.core.contracts.UniqueIdentifier;
import net.corda.core.identity.CordaX500Name;
import net.corda.core.identity.Party;
import net.corda.core.messaging.CordaRPCOps;
import net.corda.core.node.services.Vault;
import net.corda.core.node.services.vault.Builder;
import net.corda.core.node.services.vault.CriteriaExpression;
import net.corda.core.node.services.vault.QueryCriteria;
import net.corda.core.transactions.SignedTransaction;
import org.slf4j.Logger;
import org.slf4j.LoggerFactory;

import javax.ws.rs.*;
import javax.ws.rs.core.MediaType;
import javax.ws.rs.core.Response;
import java.lang.reflect.Field;
import java.util.ArrayList;
import java.util.List;

import static javax.ws.rs.core.Response.Status.*;

@Path("property")
public class PropertyTransferApi {

    static private final Logger logger = LoggerFactory.
    getLogger(PropertyTransferApi.class);

    private final CordaRPCOps rpcOps;
    private final CordaX500Name myLegalName;

    public PropertyTransferApi(CordaRPCOps rpcOps) {
        this.rpcOps = rpcOps;
        this.myLegalName = rpcOps.nodeInfo().
        getLegalIdentities().get(0).getName();
    }
```

```java
@GET
@Path("getAllCurrentPropertyDetails")
@Produces(MediaType.APPLICATION_JSON)
public List<StateAndRef<PropertyDetails>>
getAllCurrentPropertyDetails() {
    return rpcOps.vaultQuery(PropertyDetails.class).
    getStates();
}

@GET
@Path("getAllPropertyDetailsForId")
@Produces(MediaType.APPLICATION_JSON)
public List<StateAndRef<PropertyDetails>>
getAllPropertyDetailsForId(@QueryParam("id") String idString) {
    UniqueIdentifier linearId = UniqueIdentifier.Companion.
    fromString(idString);
    List<UniqueIdentifier> linearIds = new ArrayList<>();
    linearIds.add(linearId);

    QueryCriteria linearCriteriaAll = new QueryCriteria.
    LinearStateQueryCriteria(null,
            linearIds, Vault.StateStatus.ALL, null);

    return rpcOps.vaultQueryByCriteria(linearCriteriaAll,
    PropertyDetails.class).getStates();
}

/**
 * QueryableState query for retrieving property states of a
 particular price range
 */
```

```java
@GET
@Path("getBidOffersOfPriceRange")
@Produces(MediaType.APPLICATION_JSON)
public Response getBidOffersOfPriceRange
(@QueryParam("priceRange") int priceRange) throws
NoSuchFieldException {
    QueryCriteria generalCriteria = new QueryCriteria.
    VaultQueryCriteria(Vault.StateStatus.UNCONSUMED);
    Field propertyPrice = PropertyDetailsSchemaV1.
    PersistentPropertyDetails.class.getDeclaredField("property
    Price");
    CriteriaExpression statusCriteriaExpression = Builder.
    lessThanOrEqual(propertyPrice, priceRange);
    QueryCriteria statusCriteria = new QueryCriteria.VaultC
    ustomQueryCriteria(statusCriteriaExpression);
    QueryCriteria criteria = generalCriteria.
    and(statusCriteria);
    List<StateAndRef<PropertyDetails>> results = rpcOps.
    vaultQueryByCriteria(criteria, PropertyDetails.class).
    getStates();
    return Response.status(OK).entity(results).build();
}

/**
 * QueryableState Experiments ends
 */

@POST
@Path("initiate-property-transaction")
public Response initiatePropertyTransaction(PropertyDetails
Bean propertyDetailsBean) {
    Party owner = rpcOps.partiesFromName(propertyDetailsBean.
    getOwnerString(), false).iterator().next();
```

```
try {
    final SignedTransaction signedTx = rpcOps.startFlow
    Dynamic(InitiatePropertyFlow.class,
            propertyDetailsBean.getPropertyId(),
            propertyDetailsBean.getPropertyAddress(),
            propertyDetailsBean.getPropertyPrice(),
            propertyDetailsBean.getBuyerId(),
            propertyDetailsBean.getSellerId(),
            propertyDetailsBean.getUpdatedBy(),
            propertyDetailsBean.getUpdatedDateTime(),
            owner).getReturnValue().get();
    final String msg = String.format("Transaction id %s
    committed to ledger.\n", signedTx.getId());
    return Response.status(CREATED).entity(msg).build();

} catch (Throwable ex) {
    final String msg = ex.getMessage();
    logger.error(ex.getMessage(), ex);
    return Response.status(BAD_REQUEST).entity(msg).
    build();
}
}

@GET
@Path("transfer-department-to-surveyer")
//We can do so for transfer-surveyer-to-department, transfer-
department-to-bank, transfer-bank-to-department endpoints
public Response transferProperty(@QueryParam("id") String
idString, @QueryParam("newOwner") String newOwnerString) {
    UniqueIdentifier id = UniqueIdentifier.Companion.
    fromString(idString);
    Party newOwner = rpcOps.partiesFromName(newOwnerString,
    false).iterator().next();
```

```java
    try {
        final SignedTransaction signedTx = rpcOps.startFlow
        Dynamic(TransferPropertyFlow.class, id, newOwner).
        getReturnValue().get();
        final String msg = String.format("Transaction id %s
        committed to ledger.\n", signedTx.getId());
        return Response.status(CREATED).entity(msg).build();

    } catch (Throwable ex) {
        final String msg = ex.getMessage();
        logger.error(ex.getMessage(), ex);
        return Response.status(BAD_REQUEST).entity(msg).build();
    }
}

@GET
@Path("approve-bank")
public Response approveByBank(@QueryParam("id") String
idString, @QueryParam("isApproved") boolean isApproved) {
    UniqueIdentifier id = UniqueIdentifier.Companion.
    fromString(idString);
    try {
        final SignedTransaction signedTx = rpcOps.startFlow
        Dynamic(ApprovePropertyFlow.class, id, isApproved)
                .getReturnValue().get();
      final String msg = String.format("approve-bank Transaction
      id %s committed to ledger.\n", signedTx.getId());
       return Response.status(CREATED).entity(msg).build();

    } catch (Throwable ex) {
        final String msg = ex.getMessage();
        logger.error(ex.getMessage(), ex);
       return Response.status(BAD_REQUEST).entity(msg).build();
```

```
        }
    }

    @GET
    @Path("approve-surveyor")
    public Response approveBySurveyor(@QueryParam("id") String
    idString, @QueryParam("isApproved") boolean isApproved) {
        UniqueIdentifier id = UniqueIdentifier.Companion.
        fromString(idString);
        try {
            final SignedTransaction signedTx = rpcOps.startFlow
            Dynamic(ApprovePropertyFlow.class, id, isApproved)
                    .getReturnValue().get();
            final String msg = String.format("approve-surveyor
            Transaction id %s committed to ledger.\n",
            signedTx.getId());
            return Response.status(CREATED).entity(msg).build();

        } catch (Throwable ex) {
            final String msg = ex.getMessage();
            logger.error(ex.getMessage(), ex);
            return Response.status(BAD_REQUEST).entity(msg).build();
        }
    }
}
```

Now let's retrieve and test this code. First, run "gradlew clean deployNodes" followed by "build\nodes\runnodes". A series of consoles will appear, each representing a node, and this will take a few minutes to stabilize. Now using Chrome ARC, Postman, or any other REST client, send the first POST request to http://localhost:10006/api/property/initiate-property-transaction.

The request body is in Listing 4-6 and Figure 4-2.

Listing 4-6. Javascript Object Notation (JSON) request for initiating property transfer

```
{
  "ownerString": "LandDepartment",
  "propertyId": "1",
  "propertyAddress": "7 Bakers Street, London Postcode: AB1FG4",
  "propertyPrice": "150000",
  "buyerId": "1",
  "sellerId": "2",
  "updatedBy": "user11",
  "updatedDateTime": "01-01-2019:12.0.0"
}
```

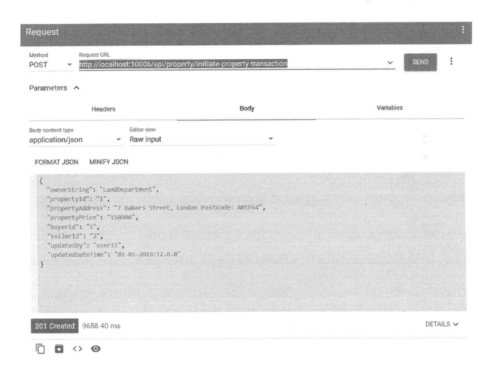

Figure 4-2. *Sending initiate-property-transaction POST request on REST client*

Now if you run the following vault query on LandDepartment node as shown in Listing 4-7.

Listing 4-7. Run Vault Query

```
run vaultQuery contractStateType: com.landRegistry.states.
PropertyDetails
```

you will get a result as in Figure 4-3.

```
Logs can be found in                    : F:\Corda\book\LandRegistry\build\nodes\LandDepartment\logs
Database connection url is              : jdbc:h2:tcp://10.0.75.1:51874/node
Advertised P2P messaging addresses      : localhost:10003
RPC connection address                  : localhost:10004
RPC admin connection address            : localhost:10005
Loaded CorDapps                         : cordapp-0.1, cordapp-contracts-states-0.1, LandRegistry-0.1, corda-core-3.1-c
rda
Node for "LandDepartment" started up and registered in 163.74 sec


Welcome to the Corda interactive shell.
Useful commands include 'help' to see what is available, and 'bye' to shut down the node.

Tue Jan 08 10:17:03 IST 2019>>> Jolokia: Agent started with URL http://127.0.0.1:7009/jolokia/
run vaultQuery contractStateType: com.landRegistry.states.PropertyDetails
{
  "states" : [ {
    "state" : {
      "data" : {
        "propertyId" : 1,
        "propertyAddress" : "7 Bakers Street, London Postcode: AB1FG4",
        "propertyPrice" : 150000,
        "buyerId" : 1,
        "sellerId" : 2,
        "owner" : "O=LandDepartment, L=London, C=GB",
        "description" : "New Property Transaction Initiated",
        "updatedBy" : "user11",
        "updatedTime" : "01-01-2019:12.0.0",
```

Figure 4-3. *Vault query result on node having permission*

However, the other nodes for the same query will give no output, as shown in Figure 4-4.

```
--- Corda Open Source 3.1-corda (d193dd8) ------------------------------------

Logs can be found in                    : F:\Corda\book\LandRegistry\build\nodes\Bank\logs
Database connection url is              : jdbc:h2:tcp://10.0.75.1:51838/node
Advertised P2P messaging addresses      : localhost:10011
RPC connection address                  : localhost:10012
RPC admin connection address            : localhost:10013
Loaded CorDapps                         : cordapp-0.1, cordapp-contracts-states-0.1, LandRegistry-0.1, corda-
rda
Node for "Bank" started up and registered in 158.6 sec


Welcome to the Corda interactive shell.
Useful commands include 'help' to see what is available, and 'bye' to shut down the node.

Tue Jan 08 10:16:47 IST 2019>>> Jolokia: Agent started with URL http://127.0.0.1:7005/jolokia/
run vaultQuery contractStateType: com.landRegistry.states.PropertyDetails
{
  "states" : [ ],
  "statesMetadata" : [ ],
  "totalStatesAvailable" : -1,
  "stateTypes" : "UNCONSUMED",
  "otherResults" : [ ]
}
```

Figure 4-4. Vault query result on node not having permission

The reason for this is the getParticipants() method, where only the owner can view the data. If your business needs other parties to view the same data, you can send the name of those parties in request and pass on to this method.

Now use the following GET request:

http://localhost:10006/api/property/getBidOffersOfPriceRange?priceRange=140000

and you will find none, whereas if you modify the priceRange as 150000 or 150001 (i.e., with a request of http://localhost:10006/api/property/getBidOffersOfPriceRange?priceRange=150000), you will find the result shown in Figure 4-5. This is a fine example of a fine-tuned query that is possible because of the implementation of *QueryableState*.

Figure 4-5. *Fine-tuned vault query result with QueryableState interface*

In the response, we can see that the owner is LandDepartment on creation. Now run a GET request as `http://localhost:10006/api/property/transfer-department-to-surveyer?id=660614e8-b441-43c3-996c-1b5518f37975&newOwner=Surveyor`, where ID is the linear ID of the first transaction.

Once this transaction is through running, "run vaultQuery contractStateType: com.landRegistry.states.PropertyDetails" will not show any result on the LandDepartment console, but it will show the whole state on the surveyor node, as the surveyor is now the new owner.

Now run the GET request on the surveyor node `http://localhost:10010/api/property/approve-surveyor?id=6efee3cb-49a9-4558-85f0-c029f32f58e2&isApproved=true` where port is 10010. You will find the "surveyorApproved" updated to true now as shown in Figure 4-6, if you vault query on the console of the surveyor node.

```
C:\Program Files\Java\jre1.8.0_144\bin\java.exe

Tue Jan 08 15:17:23 IST 2019>>> run vaultQuery contractStateType: com.landRegistry.states.PropertyDetails
{
  "states" : [ {
    "state" : {
      "data" : {
        "propertyId" : 1,
        "propertyAddress" : "7 Bakers Street, London Postcode: AB1FG4",
        "propertyPrice" : 150000,
        "buyerId" : 1,
        "sellerId" : 2,
        "owner" : "O=Surveyor, L=London, C=GB",
        "description" : "New Property Transaction Initiated",
        "updatedBy" : "user11",
        "updatedTime" : "01-01-2019:12.0.0",
        "linearId" : {
          "externalId" : null,
          "id" : "6efee3cb-49a9-4558-85f0-c029f32f58e2"
        },
        "surveyorApproved" : true,
        "mortgageApproved" : false,
        "participants" : [ "O=Surveyor, L=London, C=GB" ]
      },
      "contract" : "com.landRegistry.contracts.PropertyContract",
      "notary" : "O=Notary, L=London, C=GB",
      "encumbrance" : null,
      "constraint" : { }
    },
    "ref" : {
```

Figure 4-6. *PropertyDetails data updated after approval of surveyor*

R3 Corda Advantages

Data related to property transactions can be saved to Corda's immutable
repository, where all historical data can be tracked as and when needed.
Data can be shared only among the nodes that need to know the data. This
DApp can be integrated with a public Blockchain, where only required
data can be shared to all users as public data.

Live Implementation

Ethereum is largely used for land registry use cases across the world. However, people have started considering Corda for the same.

- As per a recent news by "Ledger Insights" (www.ledgerinsights.com/uk-land-registry-corda-blockchain-property/), "Her Majesty's Land Registry (HMLR) chose Corda for blockchain development. The project aims to explore how to make the house buying process in the UK faster, simpler and more transparent."

- Created by Bloxian Technology, "21st Century Banking" is an application that uses IBM Watson data science capabilities for finding the right home, augmented reality by Microsoft Hololens, and R3 Corda for a preauction transaction that includes the lender's commitment. The transaction also handles autobidding and settling deals in real time. Find more here: https://marketplace.r3.com/solutions/21st%20Century%20Banking/770eafff-915d-4047-b3a3-40df7ffde60a.

References

1. 21st Century Banking (https://marketplace.r3.com/solutions/21st%20Century%20Banking/770eafff-915d-4047-b3a3-40df7ffde60a)

2. Topaz (https://marketplace.r3.com/solutions/Topaz/30a79a0a-f964-42cf-a078-9d492dd2995e)

3. Dubai Land Registry Hackathon (www.hackathon.io/dubai-land1)

CHAPTER 5

Finance Domain— Real-Time e-Auction; Trade Finance and Letter of Credit

In this chapter, we will discuss real-life use cases that you can refer to for implementing in your business area. Just like Corda let's start with the finance domain, where Corda is the primary choice among DLTs for implementations in banks and the Fintech industry. Let's discuss two different use cases: e-auction and trade finance.

Real-Time e-Auction

Since the beginning of human civilization, auctions have been part of our system. An auction is the process where sellable products or services are offered for bid, and usually the highest bidder becomes the winner. The painful parts of an auction are many, and the following are some of them.

© Debajani Mohanty 2019
D. Mohanty, *R3 Corda for Architects and Developers*,
https://doi.org/10.1007/978-1-4842-4529-3_5

- There could be cancellation-related disputes, as the exchange of money and products or services does not happen in real time.

- Repudiation could also be a problem in traditional systems, as the user may claim that the bid or offer was not done by him.

- As the highest bid wins, if any user somehow misses it by a fraction of second even then the trade would not culminate. Hence, automatic settlement is a bare necessity.

- The entire auction process is not transparent, as the settlement that follows the auction is not accessible to all.

Solution

The Corda-based auction ecosystem shown in Figure 5-1 is a combination of an on-chain Corda ledger and an off-chain traditional database where we add KYC details of each of the organizations and their participants. One organization can have multiple participants, and their user IDs will be associated with every transaction that they participate in.

Real Time e-Auction

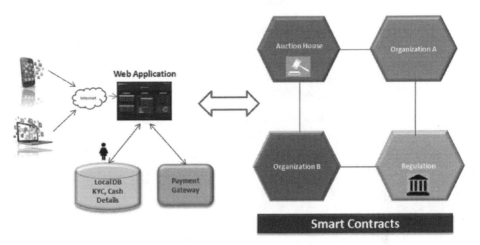

Figure 5-1. *Corda-based auction ecosystem*

The nodes/parties are as follows:

- Exchange (the auction house)

- Organization A: Can be an issuer/seller or investor/buyer

- Organization B: Can be an issuer/seller or investor/buyer

- Regulation (optional, in fact notary is doing this job for us)

Now in the beginning, the auction house will inject 100 stocks to the ecosystem. Hence, we will need to use a LinearState named *StockState*, which has the following features:

- ownerParty

- linearId

- userId

- type

133

- quantity

- offerRate

Before the auction begins, all participants in the organizations must have some deposits ready in their accounts in the off-chain database. Now Participant 1 of Organization A and Participant 2 of Organization B each have USD 1,000 in the beginning. Let's create a LinearState called **CashState** with the following properties:

- ownerParty

- linearId

- userId

- currency

- amount

- bidRate

Finally, we will create a LinearState, TradeState, which as the name signifies keeps track of all trades that will occur on the system. The following are its properties:

- linearId or tradeId

- buyerParty

- sellerParty

- buyerUserId

- sellerUserId

- cashId (linearId of CashState)

- sshareId (linearId of ShareState)

- noOfShares

- amount

- offeredRate

- bidRate

- status

- timeStamp

Now the flows will be as follows:

- ***IssueStockFlow***: To add stocks to the ledger. Here an
  output StockState is created and committed to the
  ledger. We can optionally add a regulator party who
  can check and approve or delete stocks through smart
  contract checks.

- ***IssueCashFlow***: To add cash to the ledger. Here an
  output CashState is created and committed to the
  ledger.

- ***TradeFlow***: The trade will be initiated by a participant
  from the cash issuer organization with a bidRate equal
  to or more than offeredRate, and the status will be
  "Initiated." Orders can be added or modified between
  a particular start and end time scheduled for the
  e-auction.

At the end of the e-auction time slot, the auction house will match the
orders, finalize the valid ones, and come up with the best bid rates. This
can also be done instantaneously if required.

We can add many contractual obligations, as in the following examples.
OfferedRate should be equal to or more than bidRate.

Only the highest rate among all the bidders will be chosen, and this
will culminate into a trade where the status will be updated to "Finalized."

The regulation node can check the data history and can end the
auction by updating the auction end time at any moment if things go
wrong or are out of control.

We can come up with modification and cancellation flows as per business requirements. Note that in all transactions, we have the option to use the getParticipants() method in state objects, where we can choose to broadcast the details to all the participants or do it partially.

Advantages

Instead of organizations, the preceding nodes can be representations for agencies or dealers working for a number of individual users. A user can also opt to move from one agent to another; however, all these would be an off-chain process as Corda deals only with the B2B part of the transactions. Here are a few benefits:

- Smart contracts facilitate real-time settlement of transactions

- Visibility of the entire trading cycle to each and every participant across the platform

- Auditing is made painless and superquick

- No room left for fraud because of high transparency

Live Use Cases

Though most of the live use cases are implemented on Ethereum, people have started to realize the power of Corda, which can be a best fit to give solutions for decentralized auction systems. The following sections present a few examples of how people are working on Blockchain-based e-auction systems.

- "Austria to Use Ethereum Public Blockchain to Issue $1.35 Bln in Government Bonds" (`https://cointelegraph.com/news/austria-to-use-ethereum-public-blockchain-to-issue-135-bln-in-government-bonds`)

Trade Finance and Letter of Credit

As per the World Trade Organization, in 2017 $15.5 trillion worth of
merchandise exports were transported around the world across sea, air,
rail, and road, and up to 80% of this global trade requires financing. Trade
finance involves complex cross-border trading with multiple parties
such as importers, exporters, banks, financiers, insurers, export credit
agencies, and service providers. In such a fragmented environment, many
organizations might be doing business with each other for the very first
time. As there is no central or intermediary party which can administer
the whole process, coordination is cumbersome and investment risks
are very high. It's quite unfortunate that even though trade financing
and letters of credit (LoCs) have been integral to doing business for
decades, the supporting documentation and paperwork nonetheless have
many process inefficiencies that increase costs, risks, and delays for all
participants.

In such cases, an LoC is usually used as a method of payment in
international trade, mostly to minimize the overall risk to businesses. The
entire process is represented in Figure 5-2.

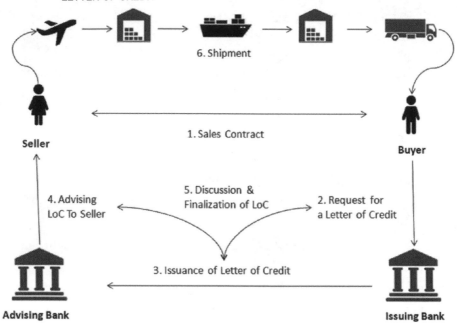

Figure 5-2.   *Trade finance and LoC work flow*

The entire process is executed as follows:

1. **Sales Contract:** Buyer (applicant/importer) from
   New York and seller (beneficiary/exporter) from
   London mutually agree to do some delivery-
   against-payment trading that involves shipping of
   deliverables among different countries.

2. **LoC Application:** Buyer gets connected to a bank in
   the UK (termed buyer's bank or issuing bank) for an
   LoC.

3. **LoC Issuance:** The issuing bank prepares and sends
   the LoC to the bank in the USA (termed seller bank
   or advising bank).

4. ***Advising LoC to Seller:*** The advising/seller bank
   does verification and discusses the same with seller
   for any modifications.

Note The beneficiary and the advising bank must be located in the
same country.

---

5. ***Finalization:*** There is a cycle here between both
   banks and buyer and seller; the LoC is finalized.

6. ***Shipment:*** Once all parties agree upon the LoC,
   the seller commences shipment of the goods as per
   the LoC contract. On delivery, the seller receives a
   delivery confirmation document. The seller provides
   that delivery confirmation receipt to the advising
   bank.

7. ***Dispatch Receipt:*** The advising bank dispatches the
   receipt to the issuing bank.

8. ***Payment at Maturity:*** The issuing bank verifies the
   delivery as per contract; if everything is fine, then
   payment is made to the advising bank.

9. ***Closure:*** The issuing bank transfers the payment to
   the seller as agreed and keeps its commission.

The preceding describes the happy path. The LoC is a contract that
gives risk coverage to both buyer and seller.

> ***Seller Protection:*** What if the buyer is unable to pay
> after delivery of goods as per contract? The issuer
> bank will do so upon the buyer's behalf as per the
> contract.

Buyer Protection: What if the seller is unable to
deliver the goods on time or up to quality? In that
case, a penalty is paid to the buyer.

Also, the preceding scenarios could be much more elaborated to
introduce prepayment and purchase order as well as the involvement of
many more parties in the supply chain space such as shipper, customs,
warehouse, insurance company, and so on.

Solution

Through Corda, we can provide a common ledger for all parties in an
LoC. Let's consider the following nodes/peers/organizations to start with.

- Buyer organization

- Issuing bank

- Seller organization

- Advising bank

- Port 1

- Port 2

First of all, we will create a LetterOfCreditApplicationState that all the
four primary stakeholders have to sign. It can have the following variables:

- IBuyer Organization (Party)

- Issuing Bank (Party)

- Seller Organization (Party)

- Advising Bank (Party)

- List of Ports (Parties)

- expiryDate

- portOfLoading

- portOfDischarge

- descriptionOfGoods

- documentsRequired

- amount

Then, another LetterOfCreditDeliveryState signifies the status of delivery of goods. This gets updated as the goods are shipped and gets loaded and unloaded port by port until they reach their destination. All stakeholders have to track this for fulfillment of the order and payment. It can have the following variables.

- Applicant (Party)

- Beneficiary (Party)

- advisingBank (Party)

- issuingBank (Party)

- status (Party)

- paymentAmount

- applicationDate

- expiryDate

- portOfLoading (Party)

- portOfDischarge (Party)

- locId

- linearId

Finally, we can have a ReceiptOfGoodsState that will be generated by
the final port where deliverable goods reach as per contract. The variables
it should contain are as follows:

- Applicant (Party)

- Beneficiary (Party)

- AdvisingBank (Party)

- IssuingBank(Party)

- timeOfDelivery

- descriptionOfDeliverables

- locId

- linearId

The flows can be as follows:

- LoCApplicationFlow: LetterOfCreditApplicationState is
  created

- LoCApprovalFlow: LetterOfCreditApplicationState is
  approved

- ShipmentFlow: LetterOfCreditDeliveryState is created
  and updated from time to time till goods reach
  destination

- PaymentFlow: LetterOfCreditDeliveryState status is
  updated with payment

Advantages

For many reasons, Corda seems to be the number-one choice among
Blockchain and DLT technologies for trade financing and LoC
applications.

- Data is private and is shared only between the nodes
  concerned with the transaction and its rightful owner.

- Blockchain reduces the overall time of settlement from
  many days to a few hours.

- Reduced risk of currency fluctuation. The payment can
  be agreed as per the date and time of delivery and as
  per the rate of international currency exchange at that
  time, which the ledger can find out on the spot.

- Fraud control, as all parties are on the same page
  and any discrepancy can easily be shared between
  concerned parties or among all parties in real time.

Live Implementations

Here are some of the live implementations of Blockchain in trade finance,
though some of them are built on other Blockchain platforms. Similar use
cases can be executed using Corda too.

- In 2016, a Blockchain-based trade finance platform was
  announced between Ornua (formerly the Irish Dairy
  Board) and Seychelles Trading Company, which was
  built on a platform developed by Israeli startup, Fintech
  Wave. With the use of Blockchain, the trading cycle of
  seven to ten days has now been reduced to less than
  four hours.

- Similarly on 6 July 2017, Japanese conglomerate
  Marubeni Corporation and Sompo Japan Nipponkoa
  established a Blockchain-based trade finance DApp
  that worked between stakeholders of two different
  countries (Australia and Japan).

143

- Danish MNC Maersk has also come up with a similar platform for shipping goods between different countries and continents.

- HSBC India and ING Bank Brussels have executed a Blockchain-enabled live trade finance transaction jointly with Reliance Industries and Tricon Energy.

References

1. Can Blockchain make Trade Finance More Inclusive? (www.r3.com/wp-content/uploads/2018/07/Can-Blockchain-Make-Trade-Finance-More-Inclusive-1.pdf)

2. Use Case - Trade Finance Letter of Credit (https://wiki.hyperledger.org/requirements/use-cases/use-case-trade-finance-letter-of-credit)

3. Letters of Credit Network (https://github.com/hyperledger/composer-sample-networks/tree/master/packages/letters-of-credit-network)

4. Letter of Credit Demo Corda (https://github.com/corda/LetterOfCredit)

5. Trade Finance and Blockchain: Three Essential Case Studies (http://cib.db.com/insights-and-initiatives/flow/trade_finance_and_the_blockchain_three_essential_case_studies.htm)

6. How Letters of Credit Work (www.thebalance.com/how-letters-of-credit-work-315201)

7. HSBC, ING Bank Execute Blockchain Transaction
   with Reliance Industries (`https://telecom.`
   `economictimes.indiatimes.com/news/hsbc-ing-`
   `bank-execute-blockchain-transaction-with-`
   `reliance-industries/66505747`)

8. Voltron, a Blockchain-Based Trade Finance
   Platform, Edges Closer to Real-World Use (`www.`
   `nasdaq.com/article/voltron-a-blockchain-`
   `based-trade-finance-platform-edges-closer-to-`
   `real-world-use-cm1052724`)

CHAPTER 6

Insurance Domain—Car Insurance

In this chapter, you will learn how the Corda distributed ledger can be used to cut downtime, cost, and middlemanship in vehicle insurance workflows, bringing transparency and expediting business processes.

Although R3 Corda started with finance-domain Blockchain projects, it gradually became the number-one distributed ledger technology (DLT) platform of choice for the insurance domain. Real-time synchronous transactions and the privacy of data by data visibility only between required nodes are just two of the features that helped Corda to quickly come into the limelight. Let's discuss a business scenario and how Corda can be fit into it.

Automobile industries mostly deal with auto insurance but also have tie-ins with service centers. In spite of the coordination, customers often have to fill out multiple forms for insurance claims and often have to wait for a longer period with little clarity on the status of the claim till it's accepted or rejected.

© Debajani Mohanty 2019
D. Mohanty, *R3 Corda for Architects and Developers*,
https://doi.org/10.1007/978-1-4842-4529-0_6

Solution

Consider the following scenario.

Imagine a buyer named Reeta visits an automobile dealer to purchase her new car. She selects her dream model and the dealer offers her an amazing deal on the new model. Also as a part of the purchase process, she's offered an insurance contract, to which she agrees and signs up for, providing her personal data along with a start and end date for the contract. When all the paperwork is complete, Reeta is given the website details to a decentralized application with credentials so she can log in at any time if she needs to file a claim. At this point, the contract is written to a block on the Blockchain to maintain the transaction.

However in a few months' time, as luck would have it, the car is stolen when she is on a road trip to a nearby town. She reports the incident to the police station nearby and then visits the provided website, logs in, describes the theft, and files her claim with the insurance company. First, an First Information Report (FIR) is processed by the police, who can either confirm or deny the theft. Let's say in this case, the theft is confirmed; the police station representative then enters all related data with the FIR reference number.

Once the insurance company monitors all active claims on the Blockchain approved by the police station, it submits a reimbursement for the claim. Just as with the previous transactions, the reimbursement is written to the Blockchain. The reimbursement can be in terms of money or else it might have tied up with a list of repair shops, had it been damage instead of theft.

Reeta is a happy customer, as she did not have to go through the painful procedure of filling out physical or e-forms again with all the same data she had provided before.

Note that insurance companies have the option to activate or deactivate certain contracts. This doesn't mean that contracts that have already been signed by customers will no longer be valid; it simply doesn't allow new signings for these types of contracts. In addition, the insurance company can create new contract templates with different terms and conditions or a different pricing structure.

As shown in Figure 6-1, the DApp will have three participating nodes or peers:

- Insurance company

- Police station

- Repair workshop

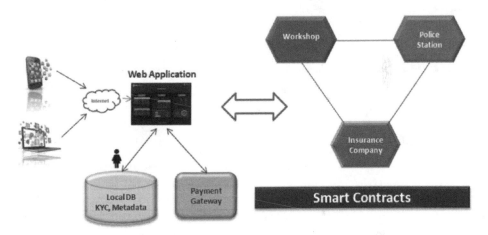

Figure 6-1. *Car insurance DApp using Corda DLT*

The automobile dealer peer sells the products to a consumer (but is not represented on this picture). The insurance peer is the company that provides insurance for the product (in our example, the car) and is responsible for processing the claims. The police peer is responsible for verifying the accident or theft claims. The repair shop peer is responsible for repairing the product.

ClaimState has the following variables:

- linearId (also the claim number)

- userId

- ownerParty

- policestationComplaintNumber

- maximumClaimAmount

- workshopEstimatedAmount

- claimState

- updatedBy

- updateTimeStamp

The flows are as follows:

- ***ClaimInitiationFlow*** – Initiated by insurance company to create a new ClaimState object and assign it to the police station.

- ***ClaimApprovalByPoliceFlow*** – ClaimState updated by the police station and assigned again to insurance company.

- ***WorkshopInitialFlow*** – Insurance company assigns the claim to a workshop, which updates the estimated amount for fixing the car. Then assigns the claim to insurance company. Insurance company approves and assigns the claim to a workshop.

- ***WorkshopFinalFlow*** – Workshop does the work and assigns ownership back to insurance company. Finally, insurance company closes the flow.

Note that the payment part is not taken care of in the preceding flows. That happens off-chain through the payment gateway.

Advantages

Insurance claims and realization often involve verification and data exchange between multiple different parties. Hence, Blockchain offers a huge opportunity here with the chance to innovate around the way data is exchanged, claims are processed, and fraud is prevented. Blockchain can bring together developers from tech companies, regulators, and insurance companies to create a valuable new insurance management asset.

Benefit to customers:

- Superior control

- Reduction in intermediary and trustless exchange

- Transparency and immutability

- Reduction of cost

- Benefit to the insurer

- Better efficiency

- Enhanced quality of service delivery while improving confidentiality and integrity of data

- Reduction in fraud

Live Implementations

Corda is the prime choice for DLT implementation across the insurance industry. There are many well-known names in the industry, such as B3i, MetLife, EY, Maersk, AIG, GuardTime, Willis, ChainThat, BlockSure, and so on, which are already associated with Corda in this space. Many are engaged with Corda for products that will hit the market soon.

References

1. Chainthat's insurance framework (`www.chainthat.com/technology/`)

2. Decentralized insurance protocol to collectively build insurance products (`https://etherisc.com/`)

3. Blockchain Accelerator for Insurance Claims Processing (`www.synechron.com/finlabs/insurance-claims-processing`)

4. Insurance Claims Processing | Synechron `www.synechron.com/insurtech/insurance-claims-processing`

5. 46 use cases (`http://dailyrevshare.com/reinsurance-process-flow-chart/`)

6. Insurance 2025 smart contracts (`http://insurancethoughtleadership.com/insurance-2025-smart-contracts/`)

7. Insurer of the future (`www.everestgrp.com/tag/blockchain/page/2/`)

8. Partnership with "BlockChain for Insurance" (`http://blockchain-insurance-summit.com`)

CHAPTER 7

Healthcare—Corda and Ethereum Hybrid Use Case

In this chapter, we will learn how an initial currency offering (ICO) through public Blockchain Ethereum can be used to pull investment from the market and how Corda can be used as a private permissioned ledger for transactions between parties. This chapter also comes with a sample project with a demonstration of attached images; this project can be downloaded by developers.

There are many different electronic medical records systems used in the healthcare industry, each with its own pattern for representing and sharing data. Such a large amount of crucial information is often scattered across multiple facilities, and sometimes it isn't accessible when it is needed most, costing money and sometimes even lives.

Portability of medical data is a huge issue, as they often fail when transferred. Everyone in the country is a patient, and many of us have had scans (MRIs or CT scans). However, where are those images stored today? CDs containing medical images are often lost. Even when patients do have their CDs, the image files frequently do not work. Also, there is often a need to transfer the existing images and all records of the patient from one

D. Mohanty, *R3 Corda for Architects and Developers*,
https://doi.org/10.1007/978-1-4842-4529-3_7

hospital to another. How can we securely pass on the data with permission from the patient without the need to generate them again and without the risk of losing the data? Let's find out.

Solution

Let's say Alice has recently founded her healthcare startup, Medison Healthcare Inc. Alice is a stalwart in the healthcare industry and has a very good network with other influencers in this business. Now she wishes to create a new Blockchain-based common platform where hospitals, labs, insurance companies, and research institutes can upload and share patient data.

Here are the different parties:

- Medison Healthcare Inc.

- Research Lab A

- Research Lab B

- Hospital A

- Hospital B

- Insurance Company A

- Insurance Company B

However, Alice does not have enough money to start her venture. Hence, she creates a white paper with the following solution to attract investors for her project through ICO.

In her solution, Alice has to create two different decentralized applications:

- An optional Ethereum-based DApp for ICO sale for collecting cryptocurrency (Ether) from potential investors, as shown in Figure 7-1.

ICO Through Ethereum Public Blockchain

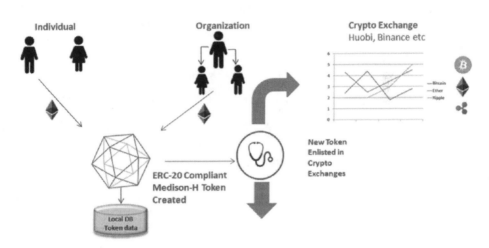

Figure 7-1. *Ethereum public Blockchain through ICO*

A new currency called "Medison-H" would be created out of those Ethers and would be registered in major crypto exchanges across the world to give good visibility to Medison Healthcare Inc. The investors, in turn, would get access to this new cryptocurrency that they can use as a discounted utility token for healthcare benefits. The token owner information would be saved to a traditional database. ICOs are simple to create. You can refer to my book *Ethereum for Architects and Developers* (Apress, 2019) for a sample ICO, or you can get loads of examples from the Internet.

- A Corda-based DApp for any kind of actual transactions with these parties, as shown in Figure 7-2.

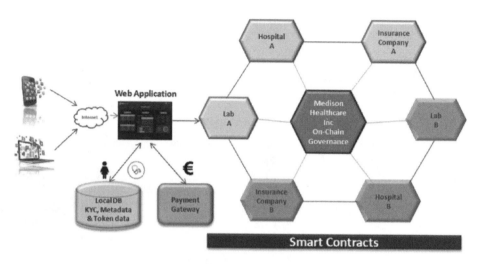

Figure 7-2. *Private permissioned DLT on Corda*

Each party will have their own node hosted in their controlled environment (Cloud or on premises). These nodes will be onboarded into the Corda network and will be a part of business network created by Medison. This will allow for the transfer of data and digital assets between communities of nodes (business networks) and different CorDapps. Relevant information can be shared between applications and organizations, creating efficiencies and avoiding duplication. The Corda network will also provide identity verification and privacy services to ensure that participants can operate on the network safely. The Corda network will be operated and managed by an independent not-for-profit organization, the Corda Network Foundation. Please refer to Figure 7-1 and 7-2, and you will see that the same local database is shared between the public and private ledgers. The Corda ledger can have access to the users who have purchased tokens. The investors with tokens would get first priority to services of the hospitals, labs, and insurance companies at a lower rate than the market. A fresh user can also use this DApp and pay regular market price for the services. This DApp can also be used as a common platform for all the parties to upgrade and share data and treat the ledger as single source of truth. Parties such as hospitals, insurance companies, and labs can get registered to this DLT after stringent KYC checks. Patients or end users can register themselves to Medison Healthcare Inc. with their token details. For convenience, I have added only two hospitals, two insurance companies, and two labs for the moment. However, in a real-life implementation, there can be many more.

Now the workflow would be as follows:

1. Shelly has registered herself with Medison Healthcare Inc. and selected her hospital, lab, and insurance company of choice.

2. Shelly is expecting her baby in a few months' time. She visits her gynecologist in Hospital A, who advises her to get an ultrasound at regular intervals.

3. Hospital A registers Shelly to the distributed ledger through its own node.

4. Every time she undergoes an ultrasound, her images are uploaded to ledger and hash saved to the PatientDataState object.

5. Also, blood and other related reports are collected from a lab and uploaded to the DApp stored against her ID.

6. Unfortunately, in the seventh month, the gynecologist finds a serious issue with the growth of the fetus and advises a cesarean section in another hospital (let's call it Hospital B) that offers a certain superspecialty.

7. Now Hospital A and Hospital B are already having some tie-ups, and they share their information with approval from the patient. The patient can be directly transferred to Hospital B and may undergo an immediate operation if needed, as all the accumulated history of documents can be availed from the decentralized ledger.

Note that we could have added the insurance company as a party as well. It's up to the business to improve this use case further. Now we can create a PatientDetailState linear state that we can share between parties. The variables would be as follows:

- patientId

- hospitalId

- labId

- insuranceCompanyId

- disease

- bloodGroup

- description

- imageId

- ownerParty

- updatedBy

- updatedTimeStamp

- linearId or patientDetailStateId

The flows would be as follows:

1. CreatePatientDataFlow – Medison Healthcare Inc. creates a new state data for Shelly with hospitalId, insuranceCompanyId, and labId as per her choice. Now the owner is Medison Healthcare Inc.

2. InitiateFlow - Hospital A updates PatientDataState with all recorded data when she visits for the first time. Now the owner is Hospital A.

3. TransferToLabFlow - Hospital A forwards the PatientDataState to Lab A.

4. LabReportFlow – The lab updates the record and sends back to the hospital. Now the owner is Hospital A.

5. TransferToHospitalFlow - Hospital A forwards the PatientDataState to Hospital B. Now the owner is Hospital B.

6. HospitalUpdateFlow – Hospital B updates PatientDataState records.

7. Insurance can be claimed by the user at any time with values stored in PatientDataState object.

Attachment

This is a special scenario where we need to use attachments.

Note   The *eHospital* project is partially implemented and can be retrieved from Apress's git location. It can be retrieved and further improved by users by adding more flows and contracts to enhance business logic.

In Listing 7-1, you will find PatientDataState.java, which is of type LinearState and stores the attachmentHashValue, which is the location of the attachment file uploaded to the node.

Listing 7-1. PatientDataState.java

```java
package com.eHospital.states;

import com.google.common.collect.ImmutableList;
import net.corda.core.contracts.LinearState;
import net.corda.core.contracts.UniqueIdentifier;
import net.corda.core.crypto.SecureHash;
import net.corda.core.identity.AbstractParty;
import net.corda.core.identity.Party;
import net.corda.core.serialization.
ConstructorForDeserialization;
import org.jetbrains.annotations.NotNull;

import java.util.List;
import java.util.Objects;

public class PatientDataState implements LinearState {
    private final Party owner;
    private final String userId;
    private final SecureHash attachmentHashValue;

    private final UniqueIdentifier linearId;

    public PatientDataState(Party owner, String userId,
    SecureHash attachmentHashValue) {
        this.owner = owner;
        this.userId = userId;
        this.attachmentHashValue = attachmentHashValue;
        this.linearId = new UniqueIdentifier();
    }
```

```java
@ConstructorForDeserialization
public PatientDataState(Party owner, String userId,
SecureHash attachmentHashValue, UniqueIdentifier linearId) {
    this.owner = owner;
    this.userId = userId;
    this.attachmentHashValue = attachmentHashValue;
    this.linearId = linearId;
}

@NotNull
@Override
public List<AbstractParty> getParticipants() {
    return ImmutableList.of(owner);
}

public Party getOwner() {
    return owner;
}

public String getUserId() {
    return userId;
}

public SecureHash getAttachmentHashValue() {
    return attachmentHashValue;
}

@NotNull
@Override
public UniqueIdentifier getLinearId() {
    return linearId;
}
```

```java
    public PatientDataState transfer(Party newOwner) {
        return new PatientDataState(newOwner,
                userId,
                attachmentHashValue,
                linearId);
    }

    @Override
    public int hashCode() {
        return Objects.hash(owner, userId, linearId);
    }
}
```

CreatePatientDataFlow.java is in Listing 7-2, where we are saving attachmentHashValue both as an attachment (so that it actually gets stored on the node) and also in the state object (so that we can retrieve the location from the linearId).

Listing 7-2. CreatePatientDataFlow.java

```java
package com.eHospital.flows;

import co.paralleluniverse.fibers.Suspendable;
import com.eHospital.contracts.EHospitalCommands;
import com.eHospital.contracts.EHospitalContract;
import com.eHospital.states.PatientDataState;
import com.google.common.collect.ImmutableList;
import net.corda.core.contracts.LinearState;
import net.corda.core.contracts.StateAndRef;
import net.corda.core.contracts.UniqueIdentifier;
import net.corda.core.crypto.SecureHash;
import net.corda.core.flows.*;
import net.corda.core.identity.AbstractParty;
import net.corda.core.identity.Party;
```

```java
import net.corda.core.node.services.vault.QueryCriteria;
import net.corda.core.transactions.SignedTransaction;
import net.corda.core.transactions.TransactionBuilder;
import net.corda.core.utilities.ProgressTracker;
import net.corda.core.utilities.ProgressTracker.Step;

@InitiatingFlow
@StartableByRPC
public class CreatePatientDataFlow extends
FlowLogic<SignedTransaction> {
    private final Party ownerHospital;
    private final String userId;
    private final SecureHash attachmentHashValue;

    private final Step GENERATING_TRANSACTION = new
    Step("Generating transaction CreatePatientDataFlow.");
    private final Step VERIFYING_TRANSACTION = new Step("Verifying
    contract constraints CreatePatientDataFlow.");
    private final Step SIGNING_TRANSACTION = new Step("Signing
    transaction with our private key CreatePatientDataFlow.");
    private final Step GATHERING_SIGS = new Step("Gathering the
    counterparty's signature CreatePatientDataFlow.") {
        @Override
        public ProgressTracker childProgressTracker() {
            return CollectSignaturesFlow.Companion.tracker();
        }
    };
    private final Step FINALISING_TRANSACTION = new
    Step("Obtaining notary signature and recording transaction
    CreatePatientDataFlow.") {
        @Override
        public ProgressTracker childProgressTracker() {
```

```
            return FinalityFlow.Companion.tracker();
    }
};

public CreatePatientDataFlow(Party ownerHospital,
                            String userId, SecureHash
                            attachmentHashValue) {
    this.ownerHospital = ownerHospital;
    this.userId = userId;
    this.attachmentHashValue = attachmentHashValue;
}

// The progress tracker checkpoints each stage of the flow
and outputs the specified messages when each
// checkpoint is reached in the code. See the
'progressTracker.currentStep' expressions within the call()
// function.
private final ProgressTracker progressTracker = new
ProgressTracker(
        GENERATING_TRANSACTION,
        SIGNING_TRANSACTION,
        FINALISING_TRANSACTION
);

@Override
public ProgressTracker getProgressTracker() {
    return progressTracker;
}

@Suspendable
public SignedTransaction call() throws FlowException {
    Party notary = getServiceHub().getNetworkMapCache().
    getNotaryIdentities().get(0);
```

```
progressTracker.setCurrentStep(GENERATING_TRANSACTION);
PatientDataState patientDataState = new
PatientDataState(ownerHospital, userId,
attachmentHashValue);

progressTracker.setCurrentStep(SIGNING_TRANSACTION);
TransactionBuilder builder = new TransactionBuilder(notary)
        .addOutputState(patientDataState,
        EHospitalContract.ID)
        .addAttachment(attachmentHashValue)
        .addCommand(new EHospitalCommands.Create(),
        getOurIdentity().getOwningKey());

progressTracker.setCurrentStep(FINALISING_TRANSACTION);
return subFlow(new com.eHospital.flows.VerifySignAndFin
aliseFlow(builder));

    }
}
```

Now in the EHospitalApi.java as shown in Listing 7-3, you can see how any file can be uploaded to a node inside the createPatientData() method. First the inputstream is uploaded to the node, which returns a SecureHash. This SecureHash is the pointer to the location of the file on the node, which is saved in the state object and also saved to the node as an attachment.

Listing 7-3. EHospitalApi.java

```
package com.eHospital.api;

import com.eHospital.flows.CreatePatientDataFlow;
import com.eHospital.states.PatientDataState;
import com.google.common.collect.ImmutableMap;
import net.corda.core.contracts.StateAndRef;
```

```java
import net.corda.core.contracts.UniqueIdentifier;
import net.corda.core.crypto.SecureHash;
import net.corda.core.identity.CordaX500Name;
import net.corda.core.identity.Party;
import net.corda.core.messaging.CordaRPCOps;
import net.corda.core.node.services.Vault;
import net.corda.core.node.services.vault.QueryCriteria;
import net.corda.core.transactions.SignedTransaction;
import org.slf4j.Logger;
import org.slf4j.LoggerFactory;

import javax.ws.rs.*;
import javax.ws.rs.core.MediaType;
import javax.ws.rs.core.Response;
import java.io.*;
import java.net.HttpURLConnection;
import java.net.URL;
import java.util.ArrayList;
import java.util.List;
import java.util.Map;

import static javax.servlet.http.HttpServletResponse.SC_OK;
import static javax.ws.rs.core.Response.Status.BAD_REQUEST;
import static javax.ws.rs.core.Response.Status.CREATED;

@Path("eHospital")
public class EHospitalApi {

    static private final Logger logger = LoggerFactory.
    getLogger(EHospitalApi.class);

    private final CordaRPCOps rpcOps;
    private final CordaX500Name myLegalName;
```

```java
public EHospitalApi(CordaRPCOps rpcOps) {
    this.rpcOps = rpcOps;
    this.myLegalName = rpcOps.nodeInfo().
    getLegalIdentities().get(0).getName();
}

@GET
@Path("me")
@Produces(MediaType.APPLICATION_JSON)
public Map<String, CordaX500Name> myIdentity() {
    return ImmutableMap.of("me", rpcOps.nodeInfo().
    getLegalIdentities().get(0).getName());
}

@GET
@Path("getAllPatientDetails")
@Produces(MediaType.APPLICATION_JSON)
public List<StateAndRef<PatientDataState>>
getAllPatientDetails() {
    return rpcOps.vaultQuery(PatientDataState.class).
    getStates();
}

@GET
@Path("trackPatientData")
@Produces(MediaType.APPLICATION_JSON)
public List<StateAndRef<PatientDataState>>
trackPatientData(@QueryParam("id") String idString) {
    UniqueIdentifier linearId = UniqueIdentifier.Companion.
    fromString(idString);
    List<UniqueIdentifier> linearIds = new ArrayList<>();
    linearIds.add(linearId);
```

```java
        QueryCriteria linearCriteriaAll = new QueryCriteria.
        LinearStateQueryCriteria(null,
                linearIds, Vault.StateStatus.ALL, null);

        return rpcOps.vaultQueryByCriteria(linearCriteriaAll,
        PatientDataState.class).getStates();
    }

    @GET
    @Path("readPatientData")
    @Consumes(MediaType.APPLICATION_JSON)
    public Response readPatientData(@QueryParam("id") String
    idString, @QueryParam("port") String port) {
        UniqueIdentifier linearId = UniqueIdentifier.Companion.
        fromString(idString);
        List<UniqueIdentifier> linearIds = new ArrayList<>();
        linearIds.add(linearId);

        QueryCriteria linearCriteriaAll = new QueryCriteria.
        LinearStateQueryCriteria(null, linearIds,
                Vault.StateStatus.ALL, null);

        PatientDataState patientDataState = rpcOps.vaultQueryBy
        Criteria(linearCriteriaAll, PatientDataState.class)
                .getStates().get(0).getState().getData();

        SecureHash secureHash = patientDataState.
        getAttachmentHashValue();
        try {
            if (rpcOps.attachmentExists(secureHash)) {
                /**Once uploaded the file can be downloaded from
                http://localhost:port/attachments/secure-hash URL
                * If we wish to share with any other Hospital we
                can download the file and send the
                createPatientData
```

```
       * request to the other Hospital*/
       URL url = new URL("http://localhost:" + port +
       "/attachments/" + secureHash.toString());
       HttpURLConnection connection =
       (HttpURLConnection) url.openConnection();
       if (connection.getResponseCode() != SC_OK) {
           System.out.println("Issue in connection");
       }
       String readStream = readStream(connection.
       getInputStream());
      FileOutputStream fos = new FileOutputStream("F:\\");
       fos.write(readStream.getBytes());
       fos.close();
    }

} catch (Exception e) {
    e.printStackTrace();
}

final String msg = String.format("File saved to path");
return Response.status(CREATED).entity(msg).build();
}

@GET
@Path("createPatientData")
@Consumes(MediaType.APPLICATION_JSON)
public Response createPatientData(@
QueryParam("hospitalName") String hospitalName, @QueryParam
                                ("userId") String userId) {
    Party owner = rpcOps.partiesFromName(hospitalName,
    false).iterator().next();
    InputStream in = null;
    File file = null;
```

```
SecureHash attachmentHashValue = null;
try {
    file = new File("F:\\testfile.zip");
    URL newFileURL = file.toURI().toURL();
    //java.io.BufferedInputStream will be created by
    openStream()
    in = newFileURL.openStream();
    attachmentHashValue = rpcOps.uploadAttachment(in);
    System.out.print("attachmentHashValue: " +
    attachmentHashValue.toString() + "\n");
} catch (Exception e) {
    e.printStackTrace();
}

try {
    final SignedTransaction signedTx = rpcOps.startFlow
    Dynamic(CreatePatientDataFlow.class, owner, userId,
            attachmentHashValue).getReturnValue().get();

    System.out.println("\nPatientDataState created with
    transaction id: " + signedTx.getId()
            + " and linear id: " + signedTx.
            getCoreTransaction().outputsOfType
            (PatientDataState.class).get(0).getLinearId()
            + " and hash: " + attachmentHashValue);

    final String msg = String.format("Linear Id: %s\n",
            signedTx.getCoreTransaction().outputsOf
            Type(PatientDataState.class).get(0).
            getLinearId() + " and attachment hash
            value:" + attachmentHashValue);
    return Response.status(CREATED).entity(msg).build();
```

```java
    } catch (Throwable ex) {
        final String msg = ex.getMessage();
        logger.error(ex.getMessage(), ex);
        return Response.status(BAD_REQUEST).entity(msg).
        build();
    }
}

private static String readStream(InputStream in) {
    StringBuilder sb = new StringBuilder();
    try (BufferedReader reader = new BufferedReader(new
    InputStreamReader(in));) {
        String nextLine = "";
        while ((nextLine = reader.readLine()) != null) {
            sb.append(nextLine);
        }
        reader.close();
    } catch (IOException e) {
        e.printStackTrace();
    }

    return sb.toString();
}

}
```

Now, first run a GET request (you can convert it to
a POST request and make the file part dynamic) from a REST client
to http://localhost:10006/api/eHospital/createPatientData?
hospitalName=HospitalA&userId=1234.

This will return the linearId and the SecureHash. Now that the file is
uploaded, it can be downloaded from http://localhost:port/
attachments/secure-hash; that is, if the SecureHash is
"E88865D1FD30B269C9C5BF9F03622039179F9D8200FC

138B2D25098815FFC2CF" and the node is running on localhost:10006, then this attachment can be downloaded from `http://localhost:10006/attachments/E88865D1FD30B269C9C5BF9F03622039179F9D8200FC138B2D25098815FFC2CF`.

You can also hit the readPatientData endpoint in another GET request to `http://localhost:10006/api/eHospital/readPatientData?id=aa3b4ef1-8adc-4738-832c-541a7903ed88&port=10006` and download the jar file in any location.

Advantages

This hybrid architecture can be used for any of the other domains discussed in this book. It comes with many benefits as follows.

- This hybrid architecture with a tokenized incentive-based model will help getting early customer engagement in business.

- We can build a secure, portable, and permanent image portability solution that leverages Blockchain technology (permissioned digital ledger).

- Using this approach, patients would never lose access to their medical images, and the chain of custody would be preserved. All historical data from all different sources can be shared between all parties as and when needed.

- The solution offers three core functionalities to enhance medical image portability and immutability (i.e., upload, storage, and retrieval at superfast speeds).

Live Implementations

Corda is mostly linked with financial and insurance domain projects, but the truth is that it can be used for any B2B Blockchain projects, including healthcare. The following are a few real scenarios where Blockchain has been used in healthcare.

- Healthureum is a new revelation in the crypto sphere that combines Blockchain and healthcare to bring the best of both under one roof. The Healthureum platform is designed on the Ethereum-based Blockchain using smart contract technology to significantly improve efficiency and interoperability of healthcare services.

- London-based Blockchain company Medicalchain signed a joint working agreement with American medical center The Mayo Clinic to use Blockchain for medical record storage.

- Led by The LinkLab and Chronicled, the MediLedger Project kicked off in 2017, successfully bringing competing pharmaceutical manufacturers and wholesalers to the same table. Together, they designed and implemented a process for using Blockchain technology to improve track-and-trace capabilities for prescription medicine.

- For full General Data Protection Regulation compliance for data.

However, all the preceding implementations are on public Blockchain ledgers as Ethereum. Corda has a huge benefit for such scenarios where data has to be protected in a DLT in a permissioned private mode and can be shared between nodes on an as-needed basis.

References

1. Blockchain in healthcare (`https://lisk.io/academy/blockchain-basics/benefits-of-blockchain/blockchain-transparency-explained`)

2. NanoHealthcareToken (`https://nhct.io/`)

3. Nano Healthcare Whitepaper (`https://s3.ap-south-1.amazonaws.com/nhct.io/NHCT_Whitepaper.pdf`)

4. corda-kyc-app Attachment demo (`https://github.com/biksen/corda-kyc-app`)

CHAPTER 8

Travel Domain: Replacing GDS with Next-Generation Travel Platform

In this chapter, we will broadly learn how airlines and global distribution systems (GDS) work and how the entire ecosystem can be greatly benefited by engaging with Corda distributed ledger technology (DLT).

Reservations with airlines, hotels, car rentals, or cruises are often associated with a third party called GDS. As per Wikipedia (`https://en.wikipedia.org/wiki/Global_distribution_system`), a GDS is "a computerised network system owned or operated by a company that enables transactions between travel industry service providers, mainly airlines, hotels, car rental companies, and travel agencies. The GDS mainly uses real-time inventory (for e.g. of available hotel rooms, flight seats, or cars) to service providers. Travel agencies traditionally relied on GDS for services, products and rates in order to provision travel-related services to the end consumers."

Well-known websites such as Expedia, CheapHotels, Discounts, Travelocity, AAA, and so on are connected to the GDS middle tier, which

© Debajani Mohanty 2019
D. Mohanty, *R3 Corda for Architects and Developers*,
https://doi.org/10.1007/978-1-4842-4529-3_8

helps to provide data for passengers to search based on their own criteria, aggregating data from hundreds or even thousands of computer reservation system (CRS) APIs exposed by many different airlines, hotels, coaches, and other travel-related organizations, as shown in Figure 8-1.

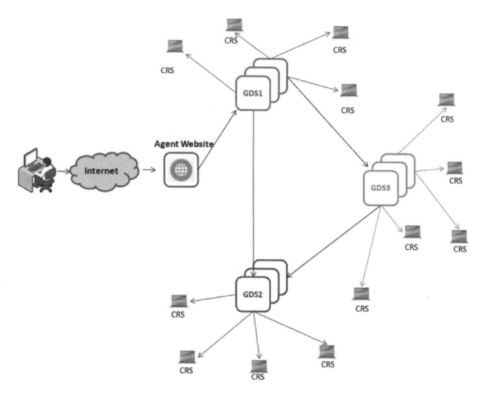

Figure 8-1. *GDS and CRS network*

For each reservation that a passenger makes, he ends up paying a considerable amount (up to 5% of the entire package in some cases) in service charges to the GDS. Also, if the GDS is hit by mistake—for example, the user tries to book a reservation but the credit card fails during the transaction for some reason—this amount is still deducted from the agent's account toward payment to the GDS. Organizations such as Winding Tree are trying to work in this area to use Blockchain or DLT to share data among all stakeholders to cut down on the cost, time, and effort of the entire transaction. However, this dream needs monumental efforts to get realized, since GDS such as Amadeus, Sabre, Galileo, and Worldspan have been connected to hundreds of airlines and innumerable hotels for decades and have been building trust that whole time.

Let's consider a scenario where a passenger has logged into an agent's website and is making a reservation that involves an airline, a hotel, and insurance. In Figure 8-2, we can observe how the entire reservation flow process works as of today. You can see that all the search activities for routes, schedules, availability, fares, and so on are gathered from cached data already stored on GDS. Once the passenger confirms and goes ahead with the reservation, the CRS or actual airline, hotel, or other related services are hit. That's also the reason why many times the actual price of the reservation varies from what we are shown during the search, as that was the stale data coming from GDS. You can view a broad representation of the entire workflow in Figure 8-2.

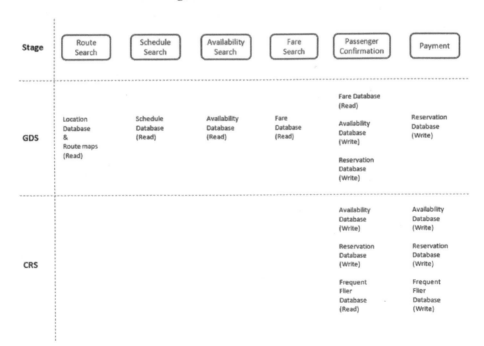

Figure 8-2. *Reservation workflow*

Solution

Now instead of a GDS hitting numerous airlines' and hotels' CRS, we will have a node for each of them, and all the data can reside on one platform. The travel agent node will carry all data related to routes, schedules, availability, fares, and so on. Every time an airline or a hotel updates any data, it will go to its own node as well as to the agent's node. Also, when we do the reservation, the data will be updated in all related nodes, including the agent's. For example, let's say an end user logs into the agent's website and searches for a package trip from Delhi to Rome. This data will come from the common database stored in the agent's node. Then he chooses a particular airline and hotel (and perhaps insurance, ground coach, etc., which are not shown here) and go ahead with the reservation. Now data will be updated in the agent node as well as in the selected airline, hotel, car rental, and all related nodes.

Let's consider the following case of a few nodes to start with as shown in Figure 8-3.

- Travel Agent
- Airline A
- Airline B
- Hotel A
- Hotel B
- Car Rental A
- Car Rental B

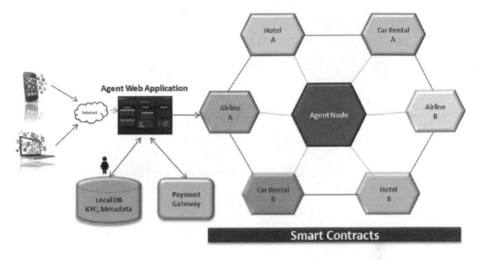

Figure 8-3. *System architecture of a GDS on Corda DLT*

The states will be broadly as follows:

- RoomDetailState

- HotelDetailState

- AircraftDetailState

- CarRentalDetailState

The flows will be broadly as follows:

- Add/update/delete search data by the airline/hotel/ground services

- Airline/hotel/ground services SearchFlow

- Airline/hotel/ground services ReservationFlow

Advantages

As per experts, GDS have been on the scene for decades and have generated trust for millions; furthermore, their coding is too complex to be handled by a DLT, or at least it's a Herculean task as of now. However, when you evaluate the advantages, you will be tempted by the following:

- Cost cutting by getting rid of middlemen in the entire claiming process

- Real-time search data and also saving of time and hassles for the end user

- Security of data, as there is no middle layer like in GDS, where there have been data attacks in the past

- The entire process is transparent for all parties involved

Live Implementations

Some of the organizations use Blockchain in travel for similar use cases; while they have mostly used Ethereum so far, Corda can also be a suitable option for such B2B DApps.

- Winding Tree: Displacing online booking hubs

- Cool Cousin: Gaining better guidance\

- Webjet: Adding assurance and avoiding inaccuracies

- Sandblock: Improving loyalty's fungibility

- Accenture: Striving toward shorter lines

- Travelchain: Making the most of data

Reference

Winding Tree White Paper (`https://windingtree.com/assets/files/White_Paper_EN.pdf`)

CHAPTER 9

Telecom Domain: Fraud Management

In this chapter, we will learn how we can control fraud in roaming services in the telecom domain by strategically engaging the Corda decentralized ledger.

Telecom is a trillion-dollar industry that often faces issues of trust and transparency. Telecommunications services involve multiple entities such as partners, vendors, customers, distributors, network providers, VAS providers, and so on. Tracking of devices is a major challenge for roaming and billing services in this industry. According to the Communications Fraud Control Association (CFCA), the loss due to fraud was almost $30 billion in 2017 and has been on the rise since then. Due to the global reach of Internet communications, telecom fraud can occur in many different forms, but let's stick to only roaming fraud for this use case.

Let's consider a case where a mobile user visits a foreign country, where the user's cell phone is under roaming. The call detail record (CDR) or data record produced by a telephone exchange is collected by the visited location's domestic operator, which is a telecom service provider located in that country. Please note that telecom companies mostly outsource data collection and billing services to third-party companies known as data clearing houses (DCHs). The user will not have access to CDRs for those roaming calls until the data arrives from the DCH weeks later, which is enough time for someone to do some sort of fraud with the roaming data.

© Debajani Mohanty 2019
D. Mohanty, *R3 Corda for Architects and Developers*,
https://doi.org/10.1007/978-1-4842-4529-3_9

Solution

A MarketWatch report says Blockchain in telecoms will become a $1 billion industry by 2023. Blockchain can help devices to be tracked on the basis of their connections to hotspots and WiFis. Also, mobile and micropayments can be made much easier with Blockchain as an alternative to established intermediaries.

Corda is a private permissioned DLT that is a perfect fit for this scenario. Telecom service providers can join this DLT after KYC verification with their roaming agreement contracts. The devices use roaming services that will be reported by other service providers and shared to the base service providers in real time. The user also can have access to this data immediately, and this will lead to fraud control and settlement of payment in considerably less time.

The following are some of the other use cases in the telecom domain that can be greatly benefited through Blockchain:

- 5G enablement

- IoT connectivity

- Identity as a service

Advantages

Some of the advantages of using of Blockchain in the telecom domain are as follows:

- Proactive prevention of fraud

- A common platform for connectivity

- Access to data in real time

- Possibility of micropayments through connected devices by peer-to-peer connection of IoT devices

Live Implementations

Some of the recent usages of Blockchain in general in the telecom industry are as follows:

- IBM and Telefónica are using Blockchain technology to build a secure network for the delivery of digital services as part of the operator's service delivery platform to improve reliability and transparency of information collected by different networks when routing international calls.

- The Viettel Enterprise Solutions Corporation, Vietnam's largest telecommunications operator and part of the Viettel Group, is using Blockchain technology to focus on providing information and communication technology solutions to the governmental and commercial sectors and to assist in building a digital government.

- South Korea's largest telephone company, the state-owned KT Corporation, is to develop a Blockchain-powered commercial network for a P2P donation platform.

References

1. SouthBlockchain for Telco (www2.deloitte.com/content/dam/Deloitte/za/Documents/technology-media-telecommunications/za_TMT_Blockchain_TelCo.pdf)

2. Blockchain Technology in the Telecom Industry (`www.rcrwireless.com/20180912/opinion/readerforum/blockchain-telecom-part3-reader-forum`)

3. Telefónica, IBM Collaborate on Telecom Blockchain (`www.sdxcentral.com/articles/news/telefonica-ibm-collaborate-on-telecom-blockchain/2018/11/`)

4. Vietnam's Largest Telecoms Company Enters Blockchain Sphere, Aims to Be Industry Leader (`https://cointelegraph.com/news/vietnams-largest-telecoms-company-enters-blockchain-sphere-aims-to-be-industry-leader`)

5. KT to Develop Blockchain-Based P2P Donation Platform (`www.zdnet.com/video/kt-to-develop-blockchain-based-p2p-donation-platform/`)

6. Blockchain for Telecom Roaming, Fraud, and Overage Management (`https://developer.ibm.com/patterns/blockchain-for-telecom-roaming-fraud-and-overage-management/`)

7. Blockchain in Telecom: Global Market to Exceed $990 Million by 2023 - Increasing Support for OSS/BSS Processes - ResearchAndMarkets.com (`www.marketwatch.com/press-release/blockchain-in-telecom-global-market-to-exceed-990-million-by-2023---increasing-support-for-ossbss-processes---researchandmarketscom-2018-07-11`)

CHAPTER 10

Supply Chain in Agriculture

In this chapter, we will explore how distributed ledger technology such as Corda can be used to bring a revolution in the agriculture supply chain, cutting down on costs, time, effort, and wastage as well as bringing transparency to the entire ecosystem.

While the IT industry is mostly focused on the banking, finance, insurance, and travel domains, whose services are mostly used by upper- and middle-class consumers, the growth of many developing countries including India is based on middle- and lower-middle-class consumers, for whom we are not producing basic items at affordable prices, which is an eternal challenge.

The Blockchain market in the government sector is expected to grow from USD 162 million in 2018 to USD 3,458.8 million by 2023, at a compound annual growth rate (CAGR) of 84.5% during the forecast period. Within agricultural supply chains, Blockchain can find quite a few rewarding use cases. The first and foremost one is in tracking and tracing the origin of food products. A study says that up to 30–40% of agricultural produce is damaged. The agriculture sector typically has very tight margins due to lack of efficient supply chain and provenance tracking, which leads to wastage and low income, in turn resulting in numerous suicides among farmers.

© Debajani Mohanty 2019
D. Mohanty, *R3 Corda for Architects and Developers*,
https://doi.org/10.1007/978-1-4842-4529-3_10

Consider the following scenario with five different parties:

- Farmers (belong to a farmer association)

- Buyers (or retailers)

- Surveyor

- Investors

- Insurance company

These parties would be working in a workflow for an agriculture supply chain scenario. Now let's find out who the parties in this use case are and what part they play in this Agritech business model:

- The farmer has farming land and skills but no money.

- The investor, who is the intermediate buyer, has a large amount of money to invest but has no farm or farming skill.

- The buyer is the actual consumer who has moderate money but has no land or farming skill.

- The insurance company provides protection to farmers.

Solution

Here is a very basic workflow in which these parties work:

1. The farmer initiates a proposal for financing.

2. The insurance company provides protection.

3. The investor agrees to buy the product at quantity, delivery time, and delivery location at agreed price A and to sell it at price B (which is more than A): the difference between A and B is the expected investor margin.

4. The buyer/retailer agrees to buy the product at agreed price A, when it is delivered at the agreed-upon quantity, delivery time, and delivery location.

5. Together, they appoint a third-party surveyor to assess the end product and provide certification.

   Now that the proposal has been created, it's time to start the real workflow for the end product.

6. The farmer starts working on the crop, which is the end product.

7. The status of the crop can be updated by the farmer from time to time to keep all stakeholders informed.

8. When the product is ready, it's delivered to the investor as per the agreed location, time, and quantity.

9. The surveyor checks the quality of the crop to provide certification.

10. The investor sells the product to the buyer as per the agreed location, time, and quantity.

11. The same or a different surveyor may again get appointed optionally to certify the final product.

There could be many different alternate flows to the preceding, but let's stick to the basic happy path for now. We can create five nodes each for a party; however, each node can be used by many different users belonging to the party with different individual IDs. For example, the node farmer is actually a farmer association that can have many different farmers, each with a separate farmer ID.

We can keep a simple state object called ProposalState. Let's say that the following are the variables we will keep in the ProposalState. This can be added to the ledger after gathering every participant's approval through a flow.

- linearId or proposalId

- cropId

- farmerId

- investorId

- buyerId

- insurerId

- quantity

- deliveryToInvestorDateTime

- deliveryToInvestorLocation

- deliveryToRetailerDateTime

- deliveryToRetailerLocation

- investorPrice

- retailerPrice

The second state object will be DeliverableState:

- deliverableId

- proposalId

- cropStatus

- isSurveyed default false

- isInsured default false

- isPaymentReceivedByFarmer default false

- isPaymentReceivedByInvestor default false

- isDeliveredToInvestor default false

- isDeliveredToRetailer default false

- isDeliveryToInvestorExpired default false

- isDeliveryToRetailerExpired default false

- updatedBy

- updatedDateTime

Now, the DeliverableFlow will be as follows:

1. DeliverableFlow will be initiated by the farmer.

2. The crop reaches the investor at the preagreed time and place.

3. The surveyor surveys and isSurveyed is set to true.

4. The investor sets isDeliveredToInvestor to true. The associate contract will also check the deliveryToInvestorDateTime from the ProposalState for successful transaction.

5. The investor pays the farmer offline.

6. The farmer sets isPaymentReceivedByFarmer to true.

7. The crop reaches the buyer or retailer at the preagreed time and place, and they set isDeliveredToRetailer to true. The associate contract will also check the deliveryToRetailerDateTime from ProposalState for a successful transaction.

8. The retailer pays the investor, and the investor sets isPaymentReceivedByInvestor to true.

The preceding is the happy path. However, if delivery to the investor or retailer is delayed (i.e., isDeliveryToInvestorExpired or isDelivery ToRetailerExpired is true) or the surveyor rejects the crop due to quality issues, then the insurer can pay for the farmer's loss. With this approach, all stakeholders can get updates on the status of deliverables on a single page. Also, the absence of intermediaries or unwanted third parties will cut down on cost and time to market and enhance the overall efficiency of the entire ecosystem.

Advantages

Please note that in the preceding example we have addressed multiple different issues of the farmers:

- ***Climate Change***

  Problem - Every year, unanticipated climate effects such flood, famine, or tornado lead to crop failures

  Solution - Efficient microinsurance products can cut down on agricultural risks

- ***Access to Farming Equipment***

  Problem - Smallholder farmer has little land and even lower revenues to invest in the machinery

  Solution – Microfinancing in the preceding model can help lenders/investors and farmers to work on a common platform

- ***Traditional Lending & Finance***

  Problem - Traditional loans are hard to come by with no credit history or collateral and when savings are minimum.

Solution – Again, microfinancing along with credit scoring can be helpful

- ***Market Access & Supply Chain***

   Problem - Multiple inefficiencies in the supply chain, due to which the farmers invariably get the short end of the stick, are far too common

   Solution – Efficient supply chain can do wonders here

In addition, we have entered only the quantity of crop in this example, not the quality. In the future, using IoT sensors, we can do the quality check as well. Smart agriculture solutions with the help of Blockchain and IoT can boost productivity and address food demand. Increased food safety and traceability, lower transaction costs and logistics issues, and new markets and business models are some of the promises that Blockchain technology make to the agriculture sector. Here are a few advantages that this emerging technology can bring in.

- With Blockchain technology, we can put all the information about the entire cycle of agricultural events onto Blockchain to enable a transparent and trusted source of information for the farmers.

- Logistically, Blockchain can speed up the movement of food through the supply chain network (critical for perishable goods), and also allow fast, targeted removal of products that are not fit for consumption. Both ways, food waste is reduced.

- Farmers can get instant data related to the seed quality, soil moisture, climate and environment, payments, demand and sale price, and so on, all at one platform.

191

- Blockchain will help in establishing a direct link between farmers and consumers/retailers, eliminating middlemen.

- The source of contaminated food items can be tracked down for food safety and control.

This will reduce the problems of low income, as Blockchain will give transparency in the supply chain, enabling farmers to get the real price for what they produce.

Live Implementations

FreshSurety, AgriDigital, HarvestMark, FoodLogicQ, and Ripe.io are some of the startups across the world that have successfully implemented Blockchain solutions for their products in AgriTech and have been awarded for their innovation. It's high time we should learn more and get empowered with these latest technologies to upgrade our age-old agriculture ecosystem.

References

1. Can Next-Generation Startups Unite Agritech and Fintech for Farmers in Emerging Markets? (NextBillion) (https://unitus.vc/updates/agritech-and-fintech-for-farmers-in-emerging-markets-nextbillion/)

2. Igrowchain (http://igrowchain.com/)

CHAPTER 11

Supply Chain—Gold Tokenization

Tokenization is the process of converting real-world securities such as as gold, oil, renewable energy, and so on to a digital equivalent and engaging it in business. In this chapter, we will discuss how distributed ledger technology can help us to tokenize gold derived from mines and involve it early in the gold trading cycle.

From the earliest years of trading, gold has secured the highest position in industry as a safe medium of investment for business tycoons throughout the world. Now let's trace the operation of the gold supply chain from mines through refineries, bullion banks, and stock exchanges, and finally to end users.

- Gold is produced by the mines in a raw form.

- Gold in its nascent form is transported to the refinery, where different grades are produced.

- Gold is checked for purity and stamped by independent surveyors.

- Refined gold reaches the bullion banks (which also work as regular banks); the bullion banks hold the gold, trade on spot, or trade at a later date per market

© Debajani Mohanty 2019
D. Mohanty, *R3 Corda for Architects and Developers*,
https://doi.org/10.1007/978-1-4842-4529-3_11

demand and supply to earn maximum profits. They offer various services such as spot trading, forwards, options, vaulting, and so on.

- Traders, jewelers, manufacturers, vaults, central banks, wholesalers, and so on purchase and sell gold through bullion banks.

- The price of gold is determined by demand and supply in the market.

Solution

Now let's see how Blockchain can be applied to the whole ecosystem.

The app will have four participants, peers, or nodes:

- Refinery

- Surveyor

- Bullion bank

- Central bank (there could be many more like trader, jeweler, vault, etc.)

Figure 11-1 depicts these flows.

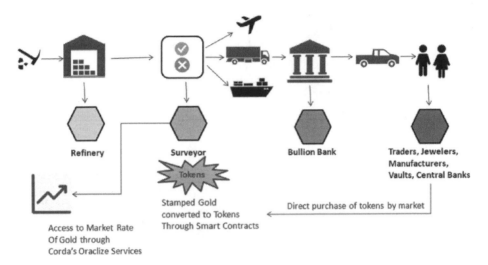

Refinery   **Surveyor**   **Bullion Bank**   **Traders, Jewelers, Manufacturers, Vaults, Central Banks**

Tokens

Access to Market Rate   Stamped Gold   Direct purchase of tokens by market
Of Gold through   converted to Tokens
Corda's Oraclize Services Through Smart Contracts

Figure 11-1. Gold tokenization

The flow of work goes as follows:

1. As a new lot of gold ore arrives, a new GoldState object is created in a CreateGoldFlow, or an existing GoldState object is updated by refinery node or weight. The state object now has information like source of origin, barcode, and so on.

2. Then, in a QualityCheckFlow, the information on the GoldState object is examined by the surveyor and a quality standard is associated with this GoldState object.

3. At this time, the current market price of gold is determined through Oracle service, and digital gold tokens are created on the ledger and updated on the GoldState object. As more and more gold is produced by mining companies, additional tokens are generated and updated, making the supply of tokens infinite.

4. Now that the physical gold has moved to the bullion bank, the owner is updated from the gold mine to the bullion bank.

5. The tokens can be sold by the bullion bank, and they can be purchased and retained by the end user at any point.

6. The token can be used as a loyalty point or utility token by the end user in this ledger as a node to buy any product/service from any other participant. The current market gold rate will not affect the trading unless the sale of gold is needed.

7. If users wish to give back the tokens and exchange them for fiat currency, they can always do so with that day's exchange rate, again by using Oracle services.

Advantages

Although ICOs are banned in some parts of the world, you can get similar benefits by using tokenization for gold, renewable energy, or many such similar use cases. Let's discuss some of their benefits.

- Tokenization helps the consumer get engaged with business and invest money early in the entire trading cycle.

- All stakeholders use Blockchain technology to automate and digitize every step in the gold supply chain.

- Peer-to-peer gold transactions provide consumers direct access to gold from the mines to the market.

- Costs are reduced for compliance, reconciliation, and transactions, enabling the trading of smaller quantities with no middleman.

- Transparency is guaranteed for all transactions, with price and location tracking and superfast settlement speed in real time via the distributed ledger.

- High-quality data protection is offered, with efficiency, control, and security and less risk of fraud.

- The outdated gold transaction model is disrupted and bypassed, which offers consumers access to gold at a market discount.

Live Implementations

People across the world have already started leveraging the benefits of using Blockchain in gold tokenization. Here are two examples:

- In June 2018, Valcambi, a precious metals refining company located in Balerna, Switzerland, entered into an agreement with Emergent Technology Holdings LP (Emergent) to use Emergent's Blockchain technology to trace the provenance of gold from mines, to the refinery, and through to vaults. Emergent's mobile application scans chips in tamper-proof seals to record the provenance of gold and the transfer of custody between participants in the gold supply chain.

- In July 2018, Emergent and Asahi Refining announced that Emergent has licensed to Asahi its Responsible Gold™ supply chain application ("Responsible Gold SCA"), a Blockchain-based technology that tracks gold provenance and movement along the supply chain.

References

1. AxisToken - Blockchain Based Solution for Logistics Industry (www.linkedin.com/pulse/axistokenblockchain-based-solution-logistics-industry-aswani-dubey/)

2. Adding Blockchain Technology, Immutability, and Traceability to Supply Chain (www.laneaxis.io/)

   - How the Gold Business Operates (www.cnbc.com/id/43974868)

   - GoldenChain (www.goldenchaintoken.org/)

   - G-Coin (www.gcoin.com/solutions/our-ecosystem/)

   - Valcambi Uses Emergent's Blockchain Technology to Further Strengthen Supply Chain Integrity (www.mining.com/web/valcambi-uses-emergents-blockchain-technology-strengthen-supply-chain-integrity/)

   - Asahi Refining Licenses Emergent Technology's Responsible Gold Supply Chain Application (www.prnewswire.com/news-releases/asahi-refining-licenses-emergent-technologys-responsible-gold-supply-chain-application-300677517.html)

CHAPTER 12

The Latest from Corda: Cordite, Corda Enterprise, and Settler

By now, I hope that you have learned how to use most of Corda's important features in different use cases. In this chapter, we'll discuss some of Corda's latest developments, such as Cordite, Corda Enterprise edition, and Corda Settler, most of which are still in beta phases undergoing updates. Hopefully, they will help industry to expedite the adoption of decentralized ledger technology by the mainstream.

Corda Enterprise Crypto Token—Cordite

In Chapter 11, we observed how tokenization is a great way to engage with clients early in ambitious ventures. A token can have a single use or multiple different uses. It can be a payment token like Bitcoin that people can use as an alternate payment medium, or it can be a utility token like a loyalty point that a user can use instead of paying fiat cash.

Ethereum made this concept extremely popular, leading to the creation of thousands of cryptocurrencies through initial currency offerings (ICOs), where established cryptocurrencies such as Ethers

© Debajani Mohanty 2019

D. Mohanty, *R3 Corda for Architects and Developers*,

https://doi.org/10.1007/978-1-4842-4529-3_12

are accepted from investors as an investment toward an upcoming business venture and a new cryptocurrency is launched, exchanged with investors, and registered in crypto-exchanges to grab worldwide public attention. Many of you might be aware that the ICO market has recently started losing its luster; but why?

- Infrastructure costs were considerable.

- Not having well-defined tokenomics and token utility led to a lack of clarity in marketing plans and campaigns.

- People started paying more attention to enterprise applications in Blockchain.

In Chapter 7, I discussed a hybrid approach in which ICO investments can be accepted in Ethers and then a Corda decentralized application can be built separately. However, we now have Cordite, a platform where ERC-20–like standard tokens can be created using Corda platform for enterprise applications in the most secure way. This approach will empower Blockchain companies to track both sides of the applications (i.e., the inflow of investments through fiat cash or cryptocurrencies) on the same ledger, rather than having one complete separate application running off-chain.

It's worth noting that the governments of many countries like India and China either completely prohibit or tightly regulate ICOs. The reason is that ICOs in their current forms are mostly archaic in nature. However, Cordite being run on Corda's private permissioned ledger can be safely used for an ICO event where only registered participants can participate, which can expand the usage of ICO crowd sales to many more regions of the world. Cordite is currently in its beta version, and its version 1 is expected to hit the market hopefully later in 2019.

Corda Enterprise

In July 2018, Corda released its first enterprise version; this version allows organizations not only to achieve the same functionalities as before, but to get the benefits of many parameters that were not present or had limited availability in Corda's community version. Apart from the same regular features, the commercial version comes with a firewall, support for Oracle and SQL server databases, capacity planning for sizing and scalability, compatibility with the community version (i.e., code tested on the community version will also work on the enterprise version), 24/7 support, and much more. This version will facilitate most of Corda's partners to expedite their new products to market and further develop their areas of business. As per Finextra News (www.finextra.com/pressarticle/74613/r3-launches-corda-enterprise): "Applications developed by partners such as Finastra, Gemalto, Guardtime, GuildOnc, TradeIX and Tradewind Markets are now live on both Corda Enterprise and Corda, serving a rapidly growing community of end users in sectors as diverse as insurance, healthcare, shipping and financial services."

Global Payments on Corda with Settler

As per open banking or PSD2 (Second Payment Services Directive) rules, the UK's nine biggest banks (HSBC, Barclays, RBS, Santander, Bank of Ireland, Allied Irish Bank, Danske, Lloyds, and Nationwide) have to expose their data in a secure, standardized form so that it can be shared between authorized organizations online with ease. It's about giving consumers more control over their data so that they can have a view of their money in all banks on a single platform, share account data details to third parties for loans or quick credit ratings, and so on.

In cross-border remittances, costs can go down dramatically and transaction times can drop from days to minutes/seconds by using Blockchain; this is one of the biggest Blockchain finance use cases. We all know that when it comes to cross-border remittances, Ripple's name comes to mind first, and Corda has already done some work in this area.

Now Corda has come up with something even more advanced: Settler.

On December 5, 2018, Corda announced the launch of a "Universal Settler Application to Facilitate Global Payments on Corda"; XRP (native currency from Ripple) is the first settlement mechanism. Corda Settler is built to ensure seamless settlement of payments on Corda across all payment schemes.

As per the announcement on Corda's website (`www.r3.com/news/r3-launches-universal-corda-settler-application/`):

> *The deployment of the Corda Settler and its support for XRP as the first settlement mechanism is an important step in showing how the powerful ecosystems cultivated by two of the world's most influential crypto and blockchain communities can work together. While the Settler will be open to all forms of crypto and traditional assets, this demonstration with XRP is the next logical step in showing how widespread acceptance and use of digital assets to transfer value and make payments can be achieved.*

—Richard Gendal Brown, Chief Technology Officer at R3

As per a tweet by XRP Research Center (`https://twitter.com/XrpCenter/status/1070334594493243392`), this is beneficial not only for Corda lovers but for XRP practitioners too. The advantages they claim are as follows:

- Second app able to settle with XRP (after xRapid)

- Development decentralization (+ arguments against security claims)

- Potential reach to 200+ tech companies and financial institutions

- Programmable settlements with XRP (Corda smart contracts)

Doesn't this look like one of the biggest news items in the world of Blockchain in 2018? Well, Settler is open source, and its code can be found on github at `https://github.com/corda/corda-settler`, all written in Kotlin. You can try your hand at this piece, and Corda claims that will soon come up with integrations with other cryptos as well as fiat currencies on Settler.

Live Implementations of Remittance

Kerala, the southernmost state of India, accounts for 35% of all foreign remittances of the country, mostly through Federal Bank, a major commercial bank in India. In October 2018, Federal Bank was in the news for building a new cross-border remittance application on Corda.

Bangalore-based Blockchain startup DigiLedge is helping Federal Bank to develop this remittance app for faster and cheaper remittances.

ICICI and Emirates NBD have already initiated cross-border remittances in October 2016.

Conclusion

Most Blockchain enthusiasts I have met so far believe that Corda is the Blockchain platform of choice for the finance and insurance domains. In truth, however, any B2B Blockchain that is on the lookout for privacy, identity/authentication, notarization, partial data visibility, multisignature support, interoperability, and so on can be used. If you need to know what organizations have used it so far to build either Proofs or real DApps, you can get a glimpse at the Corda marketplace: `https://marketplace.r3.com/dashboard`.

The Corda team has loads of plans to realize in their future releases. Here is a list of ideas: `https://docs.corda.net/head/corda-api.html`. Here, one can view the modules that are stable in production, the incubating ones expected on the market soon, and those that are unstable as of now.

The future is bright for Blockchain lovers, and that future is Corda!

References

1. 50 Use Cases (`https://medium.com/@matteozago/50-examples-of-how-blockchains-are-taking-over-the-world-4276bf488a4b`)

2. Kerala's Federal Bank Is Building Open-Source Blockchain Based Remittance App (`www.indianweb2.com/2018/10/09/keralas-federal-bank-is-building-open-source-blockchain-based-remittance-app/`)

3. Github crossBorderFundsTransfer (`https://github.com/Archstrategy/crossBorderFundsTransfer`)

4. Corda Settler (`www.r3.com/recently-released/settler/`)

5. R3 Unveils Cross-Border Payments Platform Built on Corda DLT Tech (`www.coindesk.com/r3-corda-international-payments/`)

6. Trulioo Instant Global Payments (`www.trulioo.`
    `com/blog/instant-global-payments/`)

7. Deloitte on BlockChain on Twitter (`twitter.com/`
    `Deloitte/status/866398442951778304`)

8. Oracle Sees 10% of Global GDP Stored in Blockchain
    by 2027 (`www.nextbigfuture.com/2017/10/`
    `oracle-sees-10-of-global-gdp-stored-in-`
    `blockchain-by-2027.html`)

9. Announcing Corda Settler (`https://medium.`
    `com/inside-r3/announcing-corda-settler-`
    `2287ca620f68`)

10. Banks Are Trying to Launch Crypto Assets with R3
    Tech (`www.coindesk.com/banks-trying-launch-`
    `crypto-assets-r3-blockchain-tech`)

11. The Emergence of Enterprise Tokens
    (`https://medium.com/corda/the-emergence-of-`
    `enterprise-tokens-99f6be65a3ba`)

12. Let's Talk About the Problems of ICO Marketing:
    16 Opinions (`https://hackernoon.com/lets-`
    `talk-about-the-problems-of-ico-marketing-`
    `16-opinions-ac08760af5ff`)

Index

A

Agritech business model, 186
Ariculture supply chain
    agriculture sector, 185
    Agritech business model, 186
    Blockchain technology, 191, 192
    DeliverableFlow, 189
    DeliverableState, 188–189
    IoT sensors, 191
    isDeliveryToInvestor
        Expired, 190
    isPaymentReceivedBy
        Investor, 189
    issues, 190–191
    live implementations, 192
    parties, 186
    ProposalState, 188
    workflow, 186–187
Attachment, 68
Auction, 131

B

Bitcoin, 199
    benefits, 8
    cryptology, 8
    digital wallets, 26
    execution order, 27
    hashing process, 28
    Merkle trees, 8
    miners or validators, 28
    transactions, 29
    white paper, 7
Bitcoin attacks
    consensus (*see* Consensus,
        Bitcoin)
    DDoS, 32
    double spending, 30–31
    eclipse, 32–33
    MitM, 33
    sybil, 32
Bitcoin/Ethereum, 49
Blockchain, 8, 10
    benefits, 17
    block header, 19
    defined, 10
    features, 9
    genesis block, 19, 20
    ledger, 19
    market, 185
    networks, 49, 58
Block header, 21
Broadcasting/ gossip networks, 50
B2B DApps, 180

© Debajani Mohanty 2019
D. Mohanty, *R3 Corda for Architects and Developers*,
https://doi.org/10.1007/978-1-4842-4529-3

E

Eclipse attack, 32–33

EHospitalApi.java, 165, 171

Electronic medical records systems, 153

EOS, 45

Ethereum, 23, 37, 41–43, 45

Ethereum public blockchain, 136, 155

F

Family Educational Rights and Privacy Act (FERPA), 54

Federal Information Security Management Act of 2002 (FISMA), 54

Financial crisis, 5

Flow
FinalityFlow, 69
FlowLogic, 69
InitiatedBy, 69
InitiatingFlow, 69
ProgressTracker, 70
StartableByRPC, 69
TransactionBuilder, 70

Flow list, 83, 94

Forks, Blockchain
hard forks, 38, 39
soft forks, 37

Fully centralized model, 12–14

Fully distributed model, 11–12

Functional testing, 91

through nodes, 92–94

through REST calls, 91–92

G

General Data Protection Regulation (GDPR)
Blockchain, 55, 56
compliance, 57, 59
consumer rights, 54

generateMappedObject() method, 65

Genesis blocks, 20

getParticipants() method, 63, 77, 136

Global broadcasting, 58

Global distribution systems (GDS)
advantages, 179
CRS network, 176
flows, 179
implementations, 180
nodes, 178
states, 179
system architecture, 179
uses, 175
workflow, 177

Global payments on Corda
Corda Settler, 202
cross-border remittance, 202, 203
Federal bank, 203
github, 203
UK banks, 201
XRP research center, 202

Printed in the United States
By Bookmasters